THE HORRORS OF ANDERSONVILLE

TO DENNIS,
Who has journeyed with me through all the
stories and settings

THE HORRORS OF ANDERSONVILLE

LIFE and DEATH INSIDE A CIVIL WAR PRISON

TFCB

TWENTY-FIRST CENTURY BOOKS / MINNEAPOLIS

The front cover image shows actual conditions inside Andersonville prison during August 1864, a month when more than three thousand Yankee prisoners died of starvation or disease.

The title page photograph shows a view of stockade life as seen from the main gate and was published in Harper's Weekly *in 1866.*

Twenty-First Century Books
A division of Lerner Publishing Group, Inc.
241 First Avenue North
Minneapolis, MN 55401 U.S.A.

Website address: www.lernerbooks.com

Library of Congress Cataloging-in-Publication Data

Gourley, Catherine, 1950–
    The horrors of Andersonville : life and death inside a civil war prison / by Catherine Gourley.
      p. cm.
  Includes bibliographical references and index.
   ISBN: 978-0-7613-4212-0 (lib. bdg. : alk. paper)
    1. Wirz, Henry, 1823-1865—Juvenile literature. 2. Andersonville Prison—Juvenile literature. 3. Confederate States of America. Army—Officers—Biography—Juvenile literature. 4. Prisoners of war—Georgia—Andersonville—Juvenile literature. 5. United States—History—Civil War, 1861-1865—Prisoners and prisons—Juvenile literature. 6. Wirz, Henry, 1823-1865—Trials, litigation, etc.—Juvenile literature. 7. Trials (Military offenses)—Washington (D.C.)—Juvenile literature. I. Title.
E612.A5G685 2010
973.7'82092—dc22   2008046595

Manufactured in the United States of America
1 – JR – 12/15/09

TABLE OF CONTENTS

AUTHOR'S NOTE

Thirteen thousand headstones stand within the 5-acre (2-hectare) cemetery at Andersonville, Georgia. They memorialize Union (Northern) prisoners of war who died of starvation, disease, and lack of shelter while imprisoned there.

The Confederate (Southern) prisoner-of-war camp known as Andersonville existed during the final fourteen months of the U.S. Civil War (1861–1865). When the war ended, the Union army arrested the commandant of Andersonville, Captain Henry Wirz. A military court charged Wirz with maliciously conspiring with the leaders of the Confederacy to torture and destroy the lives of thousands of Union prisoners of war. Massive numbers of prisoners under his supervision died, but what really happened inside the gates of Andersonville? Was Wirz guilty as charged? Had he, with the full knowledge and approval of the Confederacy, intentionally starved and withheld medical treatment from Union prisoners? Or did other factors contribute to the suffering?

At the time, a few voices, though not many, suggested that the Union could have saved their men but chose not to. In the months and years that immediately followed the Civil War, the idea that a government would deliberately sacrifice its own men was viewed as outrageous. But as years became decades and the passions of war cooled, the truth about Andersonville began to emerge.

In telling this story of Andersonville, I have researched the memoirs of many soldiers who survived the camp. I have relied also on key Civil War government documents compiled as the Official Records of the War of the Rebellion (commonly referred to as ORs). These records include official military communications and reports. They were compiled by the U.S. government in the decades after the War of Rebellion, another name for the Civil War. I also extensively used the media of the times—primarily newspaper and magazine articles—not only for text to a simple narrative of good versus evil. Nor is it a story of North versus South. Rather, it is an examination of how, within months, conditions inside a prisoner-of-war camp deteriorated to the point where hundreds died daily.

> ULTIMATELY, THIS IS A STORY OF SURVIVAL—OF HUMAN CRUELTY, YES, BUT ALSO HUMAN KINDNESS AND COURAGE.

references but also for illustrations and photographs. But not every source is accurate. Often I discovered different versions of the same event. I uncovered bias and anger in the articles of reputable news publications and even in the sworn testimony of witnesses. I read the transcript of the trial of Henry Wirz, looking for truth and fiction in the accusations made against the man who became the scapegoat for the suffering that took place within the prison.

After two years of research, I understood that the story of Andersonville could not be reduced It is not the story of a single man who deliberately inflicted suffering on the enemy. Rather, it is a story of many men whose lives became a tangled knot of misfortune and misery. Ultimately, this is a story of survival—of human cruelty, yes, but also human kindness and courage.

The nonfiction writer's challenge is not only to find information but to interpret it in a fair way. I hope I have achieved this. I hope, too, that my readers will understand that the story of a war goes far beyond what happens on the battlefield.

CATHERINE GOURLEY

UNION SOLDIERS

DORENCE ATWATER was sixteen when he enlisted in the army in 1863. Months later, he became a prisoner of war and was eventually sent to Andersonville. Atwater's job in camp was to make a daily record of the names of the Union soldiers who died in the prison.

WILLIAM COLLINS, a soldier from Pennsylvania, became a prisoner of war in 1863. While a prisoner at Andersonville, he organized a gang of thugs called the Raiders. They stole food and clothing from weak or dying prisoners.

JOHN McELROY was sixteen when he enlisted in the Illinois Cavalry in 1862. In January 1864, the Confederates captured McElroy and sent him to Andersonville. He later wrote a memoir of his fourteen months as a prisoner of war there.

JAMES MADISON PAGE, a soldier in the 6th Michigan Cavalry, became a prisoner of war in 1863. For seven months, he was held inside Andersonville. Decades after the war, Page wrote a book about Henry Wirz.

JOHN RANSOM enlisted in the 9th Michigan Cavalry. A prisoner of war from 1863 until 1864 at both Belle Isle and Andersonville, John Ransom kept a diary that detailed the horrors of his experience at Andersonville.

JOHN W. URBAN (also known as John Dowd) enlisted in the 2nd Pennsylvania Infantry in 1861. Taken prisoner in June 1864 and sent to Andersonville, Urban was robbed and severely beaten in the camp by members of the Raiders.

CONFEDERATE SOLDIERS

BRIGADIER GENERAL JOHN H. WINDER was the Confederate officer in charge of Union prisoners of war east of the Mississippi River, including the Andersonville camp.

CAPTAIN RICHARD WINDER was the nephew of Brigadier General John H. Winder, who assigned him to oversee supplies at Andersonville.

CAPTAIN HENRY WIRZ, commandant of Camp Sumter, also known as Andersonville prisoner-of-war camp, was responsible for managing the inside of the facility.

INDIVIDUALS ASSOCIATED WITH THE WIRZ COMMISSION

LIEUTENANT COLONEL NORTON P. CHIPMAN was the judge advocate who served as the prosecuting attorney in the 1865 Wirz court-martial.

LOUIS SCHADE AND **ORRIN BAKER** were the attorneys who defended Wirz during his trial.

MAJOR GENERAL LEW WALLACE was the president of the military tribunal that court-martialed Wirz.

CAPTURED!

James Madison Page was a Union soldier in the 6th Michigan Cavalry. On the sleeve of his blue uniform, he wore the stripes of a commissary sergeant. He was not a combat soldier. He did not fix a bayonet onto his rifle and charge into battle on horseback as the other cavalry soldiers did. His responsibilities were to manage and distribute the supplies—food and blankets—as the soldiers advanced on and skirmished with the enemy.

Although his was the lowest rank of sergeant, Page dreamed one day of becoming a war hero. His fantasy was to capture one of the Confederacy's most notorious officers, Colonel John S. Mosby. In the hills and ravines of Virginia, Mosby and his rebel (Confederate) raiders tormented Union troops. They struck without warning and disappeared in the countryside like shadows.

The fantasy ended on September 21, 1863, along the banks of the Rapidan River near the town of Liberty Mills, Virginia. Page and the other soldiers in his company were advancing slowly through a field of corn shocks. The harvested and stacked corn provided some cover as they climbed a small elevation. Page had strayed away from the others. When he reached the top of the hill, he saw at once that his company was doomed. Below and marching toward them, "as if on parade," were several hundred Confederate troops.

Page turned and fled, crashing downhill toward the safety of the river. Greatly outnumbered, the Union troops—Page among them— never made it that far. His Confederate captors found him hiding in the tall grass. James Madison Page had become a prisoner of war.

Six weeks later, John Ransom suffered a similar fate. He, too, was a commissary. On the evening of November 5, 1863, the 9th Michigan

Prisoner James Madison Page was one of more than ninety thousand troops sent by the state of Michigan to fight with the North during the Civil War. The photo shows the officers of a Michigan infantry unit in 1861.

Cavalry encamped in a bend of the Holston River in eastern Tennessee. A chilling rain fell all night, miring the roads in mud. Before dawn, the commanding Union officer put forth an order to break camp immediately. John Ransom didn't hesitate. Within ten minutes, he had managed to get the mules and the army wagon train in line on the road. Even so, the alarm had come too late. The Union soldiers soon realized they were surrounded by Confederate rebels.

Although the soldiers returned fire, the surprise attack at dawn had sealed their fate. The Confederate troops seized the mules and wagon train, including its stores of clothing and food. Hundreds of the Michigan soldiers died or were wounded in the battle. By nightfall the Union soldiers had surrendered. Twenty-year-old John Ransom was a prisoner of war.

In the autumn of 1863, prisoner-of-war trains brought both James Page and John Ransom to Richmond, Virginia—the capital of the Confederacy. A year earlier, boisterous voices had taunted blue-coated Yankee (Union) prisoners as their Confederate captors marched them through the city's streets. Those voices were silent now. After two years of war between the North and the South, the city's residents were weary. So many bluecoats had been taken prisoner that another boxcar of Yankees was of little interest.

In 1861 Confederate president Jefferson Davis and his young family moved into this Richmond, Virginia, home. The structure, which became known as the White House of the Confederacy, still exists as part of Richmond's Museum of the Confederacy.

PART 1: THE CAMP

DECEMBER 1863 TO NOVEMBER 1864

CHAPTER ONE
ON BELLE ISLE

It is of the nature of the prisoner's condition that he should share the lot of those with whom he is a prisoner. He cannot expect better fare than that which is received by the soldiers to whom he surrenders. If they pine for want, then he must pine too. If they live plentifully, he must be fed plentifully also. If one party or the other suffers, he must be that party.

—*RICHMOND DISPATCH,*
DECEMBER 27, 1863

Upon reaching Richmond, the Yankee enlisted men were taken directly to Belle Isle, a 54-acre (22-hectare) island in the James River.

John Ransom removed the small book he kept tucked inside his clothing. On a blank page, he recorded the date: December 1, 1863. "Very hungry and am not having a good time of it," he wrote.

John Ransom was in a Confederate prison on Belle Isle in the middle of the James River at Richmond. A single bridge connected the island to the mainland, so Belle Isle was a secure location for a prisoner-of-war camp. The camp had no barracks. Instead, the Confederate army had erected Sibley tents for the captive Yankees. Each of these circular shelters, about 18 feet (5.5 meters) in diam-

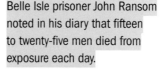

Belle Isle prisoner John Ransom noted in his diary that fifteen to twenty-five men died from exposure each day.

eter, was held up by a single pole that raised the tent to a central peak. By December 1863, more than ten thousand Union prisoners were on the island. Without enough of these tents for shelter, the prisoners were crammed into the Sibleys well beyond their twelve-person capacity. Newcomers were forced to sleep out in the open. At night, fog off the river blanketed Belle Isle. The prisoners paced to keep warm, walking until too weak to stand. Some cried "like little children," Ransom wrote in his diary. He noted, too, that a soldier lying near him had frozen to death during the night. All the next day, the body had remained on the ground. Before dark, Confederate guards finally carried the corpse out of camp, "feet foremost."

A few days later, on December 6, 1863, Ransom cursed in his diary about ever having enlisted in the army. Still, he was one of the lucky ones. He was alive. And he had a blanket.

Prisoner James Page had neither tent nor blanket. His survival depended on his "boys," the eleven men from his regiment who had been captured together. On Belle Isle, the Michigan 11 looked out for one another. A loyal comrade was as good as or even better than a Sibley tent. For example, when Page developed a fever, his boys managed to secure some canvas to wrap around him to keep him warm. They shared their rations with him, nursing him until he could walk again. A Confederate guard gave him an apple—a kindness that Page never forgot. As hungry as he was, he shared that apple with his regiment boys.

Once he had recovered, Page created a sort of market business on Belle Isle. He sold his watch to a guard in exchange for sausages, biscuits, and tobacco. He cut up the sausage into bites and pinched the tobacco into plugs to chew. Each day he walked up and down the prison's makeshift street, asking ten cents (or a dollar in Confederate money) for a piece of sausage or a plug of tobacco. The business kept his brain busy, he said. And a healthy mind was as important to survival as a healthy body. James Page intended to leave Belle Isle one day—and not feetfirst.

⊰══◉══⊱

Brick warehouses lined the shore of Richmond's James River. Before the war, these buildings had held tobacco, bushels of corn and wheat, and bales of cotton—cash crops that were loaded onto ships and sent to factories in the North or across the Atlantic Ocean to the United Kingdom and France. The three-story building rising above a canal on the corner of Carey and 20th streets was L. Libby & Son, Ship Chandlers. Before the war, Luther Libby had sold shipping supplies such as barrels and tarred rope. Soon after the war began, the Confederacy converted the Libby building and its surrounding warehouses into a prison. Unlike the soldiers on Belle Isle, who were enlisted men (privates and sergeants), the Yankees in the Libby prison were officers—lieutenants, captains, majors, colonels, and generals.

At fifty-nine years, Brigadier General Neal Dow was one of the oldest and highest-ranking Union prisoners of war. At the Libby prison, he lived as the other officers did, crowded into the low-ceilinged rooms that had plank floors and brick walls. The barred windows had no glass

A lithograph shows the exterior of Richmond's Libby Prison as it appeared in August 1863. A former warehouse, the building provided a degree of shelter for captured Yankee officers.

to block the winter winds off the river. Each day Dow gazed through the window of his cell. He could see the boats on the canal below. Aboard those vessels, the general knew, were tins of coffee, tea, sugar, salted beef and ham, molasses, and jelly preserves.

The Confederate War Department did not have large quantities of food for its own soldiers—much less for its prisoners of war. So charities and families of Union prisoners shipped food to Richmond to feed the hungry prisoners. But often weeks would pass before Confederate guards unloaded the boxes and delivered them. Some prisoners complained that the guards went through their packages, taking what they wanted for themselves.

Before enlisting in the Union army, Brigadier General Neal Dow had been the mayor of Portland, Maine.

From his window, Dow could also make out the peaks of the Sibley tents on Belle Isle. Months earlier, his captors had allowed him to cross the long bridge to the island to distribute supplies sent from the North to the enlisted men. However, he had strongly criticized the poor rations and the unhealthy conditions on Belle Isle and was no longer allowed to leave the Libby.

Like John Ransom, the general kept a diary. That winter of 1863, he wrote, "Our men at Belle Isle are suffering a slow starvation. . . . And after a cold night, some of them are found dead. They lie in the trench that surrounds the camp." Although Dow could no longer help those enlisted men, he asked the Reverend John Hussey to see what he could do. As a volunteer for the U.S. Christian Commission, Hussey visited prison camps and distributed food and clothing. In November 1863, he had spent three days visiting the imprisoned Union officers in the Libby. On Dow's request, he had also walked the long bridge across the river to Belle Isle. He later reported on the conditions he found there:

> *The rations are, for each man, twelve ounces [340 grams] of bread and two to three ounces [56 to 85 g] of beef or mutton in twenty-four hours, given about 1 o'clock each day, and nothing else; no stoves, no fuel, no light at night, no soap. They have no straw or bunks and very insufficient clothing and blankets; not one in four has a blanket. They have very generally bad colds and cough incessantly. They are not allowed to purchase anything. What they get is got by stealth from the guard.*

Feeding the growing number of Union prisoners was a problem for the Confederacy, whose army was already on reduced rations. Even the army's horses were suffering. In November 1863, the commander of the Army of Northern Virginia, General Robert E. Lee, had sent an urgent message to the Confederate War Department. In the last five days, Lee reported, he had received only 3 pounds (1.3 kilograms) of corn per horse from Richmond. General Lee depended on Richmond to supply his troops as well as his horses. "At this rate, the horses will die, and cannot do hard work," he wrote.

Robert E. Lee was a brigadier general and later a full general, in charge of the Army of Northern Virginia. In January 1865, he was made commander in chief of the Confederate armies, a title he held briefly. In April of that same year, he surrendered to General Ulysses Grant at Appomattox.

THE "SO-CALLED CONFEDERACY"

From December 1860 through May 1861, thirteen Southern states had declared their independence from the federal government of the United States of America. They formed a new government and a new nation, the Confederate States of America. The CSA, or Confederacy, elected representatives to serve in this government. The Confederacy adopted a new constitution and elected as president Jefferson Davis, who lived in a mansion in Richmond. The Confederacy printed its own money. And the Confederacy called its citizens to arms. Men from all Southern states rallied around the Confederate flag, nicknamed the Stars and Bars, ready to defend their new country from the invasion of the Federals in the North.

Northern leaders never recognized the Confederacy as an independent nation. There was only one Constitution for the United States, and it did not allow any state to simply quit the Union. This "so-called Confederacy," as Northern newspapers frequently referred to the CSA, was illegal and would not be tolerated. The North believed the rebellion of the Southern states had to be suppressed.

More than two years of war had changed the Virginia landscape. Fertile farmlands had become battlefields. Foraging armies had harvested crops or burned them to starve out the enemy. Roads and railroads had been destroyed in battle so farmers who did manage to raise crops could not transport them to nearby cities. As a result, food often rotted in storehouses along railroad platforms.

On Belle Isle, in the prison warehouses along the James River, on the battlefields of Virginia—hunger was war's companion. Even in Richmond, mothers struggled to feed their families. John B. Jones, a

Damaged railroad tracks throughout Virginia made it difficult for farmers to send their food to the cities, most of which were suffering severe shortages.

clerk in the Confederate War Department, noted in his diary in 1863 that dinner was often just an egg with corn bread, rice, and potatoes but no meat. His daughter's thin arms filled him with despair. How much longer might the war continue? Jones wondered. Another year? Two? If so, he feared that famine—and not Yankee soldiers—would bring the South to its knees.

The Confederate officer in charge of all prisoners of war in Richmond was General John H. Winder. Winder was in his sixties, a white-haired, stocky man who had served in the U.S. Army for decades before the war. As the Confederate provost marshal (military police chief) of Richmond, Winder had an important assignment. Richmond was the political and military heart of the Confederacy. President Davis met with representatives of the new congress in Richmond, and the War Department conducted business there.

BLOCKADE-RUNNERS

To starve the South into surrender, the North imposed a blockade of Southern ports during the Civil War. The Union navy patrolled the seaways off the Confederacy's Atlantic coast. The patrol's mission was to prevent Confederate ships from entering or departing its harbors. The blockade prevented more than just food and medicine from entering the Confederacy. Badly needed resources such as coal and iron ore to manufacture weapons and to repair railroad tracks and locomotives also became scarce. The blockade also made it difficult for the Confederate government to ship its cash crops (tobacco and cotton) to other nations for badly needed cash.

Blockade-runners were fast ships that often succeeded in eluding the Union patrols. Their captains were heroes throughout the South. But when the goods did make it into the Confederacy, too often they ended up in the hands of war speculators. The speculators hoarded everything from beef and butter to coffee and tea. They sold the items at exorbitant prices. Butter, which might have sold for ten or twenty cents a pound (0.5 kg) before the war, had soared to $3.50. But few average citizens could afford such luxury. John B. Jones, a clerk for the Confederate War Department in Richmond, noted in his diary in 1863 that his wife had succeeded in purchasing a barrel of flour for $28—more than twice what it might have cost a year earlier. It was a high price, but a family still had to eat.

The *Teaser*, a Confederate blockade-runner, sails off Fort Monroe, Virginia, in December 1864.

Winder's role in maintaining law and order in the city and in its prison camps was critical for the survival of the Confederacy.

Although Winder had the confidence and support of Davis, many residents of Richmond viewed the old general as a tyrant. He hired detectives, reputed to be thugs, to ferret out Union spies who might be living in or passing through the capital. He closed saloons and prohibited the sale of alcohol. He enforced the use of military passes to control who entered and left the city. Some people believed Winder treated the residents of Richmond more harshly than he did the Yankee bluecoats on Belle Isle. One news correspondent said Winder's gray eyes were "cold, cruel" and he had a "haughty, insulting air." The correspondent found it easy to believe what many people in Richmond had said about the general, that he was "unrelenting" and "heartless."

Earlier in the year, General Winder had cut rations for the prisoners to basic sustenance. But by 1863, hundreds of new bluecoat prisoners were arriving, sometimes daily. The military commissary could not supply even the bare minimum to keep prisoners alive. Winder had no choice but to use some of the barrels of flour intended for Richmond's citizens to feed the prisoners. This angered many residents, but the general paid little attention. He had no kindness in his heart for Yankees. But he did know this: hungry men are dangerous men.

⊷═◎⊜⊷

The prisoners on Belle Isle crowded around the newest arrivals to camp. They were hungry for information. They asked about news of regiments and of exchange.

Exchange. Every prisoner longed for it. Exchange meant leaving Belle Isle under a flag of truce and returning home. In exchange, a Southerner would be released from a Northern prison. Soldiers who had been in prison for weeks or months felt certain their government would act soon to secure their release. It was just a matter of time—a few days or a few weeks more—until they were free.

⊷⊜⊶

"Christmas.—Cold, last night. Cloudy and cold to day," wrote Dow in his diary. "No fuel—the tables and benches are broken up. For cooking! The Confederacy too poor—really have no wood, they say."

On Belle Isle, Ransom lay wrapped in his blanket, listening to the church bells of Richmond. He remembered Christmas one year ago, feasting on beef and crackers with butter, oysters, and cheese. On this Christmas day, Ransom received no rations. Still, he was hopeful. "There are better days coming."

> SOLDIERS WHO HAD BEEN IN PRISON FOR WEEKS OR MONTHS FELT CERTAIN THEIR GOVERNMENT WOULD ACT SOON TO SECURE THEIR RELEASE.

Elsewhere in the island prison, Page huddled with his boys. William (Billy) Bowles, one of the Michigan 11, kept up his spirits by cursing the Southern Confederacy, the U.S. secretary of war Edwin M. Stanton, and President Abraham Lincoln and the rest of them in Washington, D.C., who had sent them here to suffer. Then Bowles got an idea. He gathered his comrades. He promised to treat them to a Christmas dinner feast as soon as they were exchanged—no matter what day or month it was. He found a piece of paper and asked each man what he would like to eat for that dinner.

Although their relationship was often stormy, President Abraham Lincoln *(left)* and his secretary of war Edwin M. Stanton shared the painful burden of conducting a war against their ex-citizens.

Oysters said one. Roast beef said another. Turkey, ham, and plum pudding—Bowles wrote down each item next to the man's name. Just imagining the feast brought tears to the eyes of most, said Page. On the top of the list, Bowles wrote: "Bill of fare that we didn't get at Belle Isle, on Christmas, 1863." And he vowed to keep his word.

Although they did not know it then, their stay on Belle Isle was nearly over. Before long, Ransom and Page and many thousands more would walk across the long bridge to Richmond—but not to freedom. Their destination was not their home in the North but a small town in the Georgia wilderness called Americus.

CHAPTER TWO

THE ROAD TO AMERICUS

It will not be long ere [before] many of the Yankee prisoners, now in confinement on Belle Isle, will have an opportunity of breathing the salubrious [healthy] air farther South, the Government having made selection of a spot in Georgia, near Andersonville, Sumtar county, for their reception and safe-keeping, their present place of confinement being rather over-crowded. The location is on the Southwestern railroad, between Oglethorpe and Americus, where no difficulty will be encountered in supplying their wants.

—"CHANGE OF BASE," *RICHMOND SENTINEL*,
DECEMBER 30, 1863

The editors of the *Richmond Enquirer* concluded in February 1864 that officials at the Confederate War Department were either "heedless or ignorant" of the seriousness of the overcrowding at the Libby. The warehouses were so tightly packed with prisoners that a news reporter wondered why bodies weren't tumbling out of the warehouse windows. The crowded conditions of the enlisted men held prisoner on Belle Isle also concerned the citizens of Richmond, but not because the men lacked food and shelter. Mostly the people feared the men would escape across the long bridge and ravage the town.

In fact, the War Department was much aware of the overcrowding and had initiated a plan the previous November to address the situation. The Confederate secretary of war, James A. Seddon, ordered General Winder to find a suitable location for a new prisoner-of-war camp farther south, perhaps in the interior of Georgia. The secretary had specific requirements.

First, the location had to be isolated so that raids from Union troops to free their comrades would be unlikely and escapees would not be able to return to Union lines. Second, the location had to be accessible by railroad so that prisoners and supplies could easily be transported there. Finally, the land chosen should have plenty of space, a supply of clean water, and abundant resources—timber for building barracks and farmland for growing wheat and corn to feed the men.

Soon after receiving the order, General Winder immediately assigned his own son, Captain Charles Sidney Winder, to fulfill the secretary of war's request. A few days later, Captain Winder arrived in Americus, the capital of Sumter County. In addition to a courthouse, the town had a few Baptist churches and stores that served nearby farmers and farm laborers.

No battles had been fought in Americus. Even so, the war had changed lives there. Many young men from the area had enlisted in the Confederate army. Most fought with the army in Virginia. Others were fighting in Tennessee. The local newspapers

James A. Seddon *(above)* was the third of President Jefferson Davis's four secretaries of war, serving from 1862 to 1865. Captain Charles Sidney Winder *(below)*, a West Point graduate, was the youngest man ever to be appointed captain. He resigned his commission in 1861 to join the Confederate army.

published articles about the battles and occasionally reprinted letters the soldiers had written to their families. Patriotism for the Confederacy was high. But the people of Americus were not particularly happy with the idea of thousands of Union prisoners living near their homes.

Captain Winder and a Confederate agent in charge of supplies in southwestern Georgia rented a wagon to investigate a location 11 miles (18 kilometers) northwest of Americus—a whistle-stop called Anderson Station on the Central of Georgia railway. A whistle-stop usually refers to a small town along a railroad line. Rather than making a scheduled stop at these stations, the train stops only when the station's whistle sounds, indicating a waiting passenger or freight shipment. Anderson Station was not a town or even a village. It was a seldom-used stretch of track that allowed trains on the same line to pass one another. A single log building stood alongside the track, and only a few families lived nearby. The secretary of war had specified an isolated location. Without a doubt, Anderson Station fit the bill.

The station agent in charge of Anderson Station was Ben Dykes. His brothers were fighting in the Confederate army, but Ben was lame and unfit for military service. Land approximately one-quarter mile

The Andersonville depot photographed after the war shows an area full of activity, but it was a desolate track through the wilderness when the Yankee prisoners first arrived.

(0.4 km) east of the station belonged to him. He would be more than willing to lease the land to the Confederate government for a prison camp.

Dykes escorted Captain Winder to the site, which had plenty of tall pine trees but no streams for water. Nearby, however, was a clearing that sloped down to a branch of the Sweetwater Creek flowing through another parcel of land, this owned by a local man named Wesley Turner. The marshy land along the creek supported a few sweet gum trees, some creeping vines, and some plants. Fleas burrowed in the sandy soil. In summer the low, swampy land would breed swarms of mosquitoes and flies.

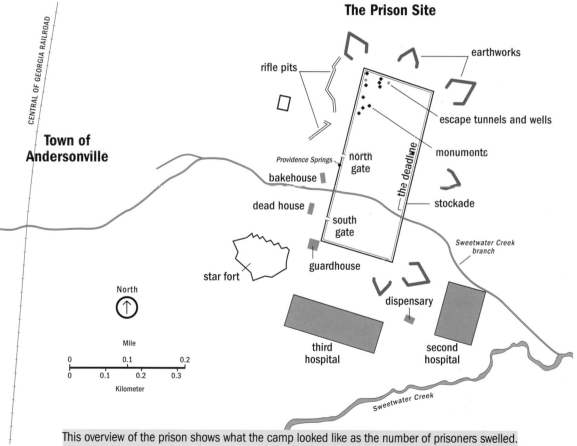

The Prison Site

CENTRAL OF GEORGIA RAILROAD

Town of Andersonville

rifle pits

earthworks

escape tunnels and wells

Providence Springs

north gate

the deadline

monuments

bakehouse

dead house

stockade

south gate

Sweetwater Creek branch

star fort

guardhouse

dispensary

North

third hospital

second hospital

Mile

0   0.1   0.2

0   0.1   0.2   0.3

Kilometer

Sweetwater Creek

This overview of the prison shows what the camp looked like as the number of prisoners swelled. Buildings around the camp, such as hospitals, were added as more and more Union soldiers arrived.

For Captain Winder, the decision came down to two things: land and water. The camp needed both. And so he made agreements with Turner and Dykes to lease both parcels of land.

Far north in New York City, the editors of the *New York Times* learned of the Confederacy plan to construct a new prisoner-of-war camp in Georgia. In an article, "Where Our Prisoners Are Going," the newspaper described the site as a place that offered little more than "fish, fever, and alligators." And yet, the editors saw something positive. The choice of such an inferior parcel of land indicated just how desperately trapped the Confederacy was. "From Andersonville the prisoners can only be removed, for further safety, to the swamps of Georgia and Florida."

General Winder used his influence with the Confederate secretary of war to appoint his nephew as quartermaster (officer in charge of food, clothing, and other supplies) of the new camp in Georgia. Captain Richard Winder received his orders in December 1863 and traveled at once to Americus. His first task was to build the camp itself.

Like his cousin Sidney, Richard Winder discovered that the local people in Americus were opposed to the prison. They refused to assist in clearing the land and building and would not even provide mules, wagons, shovels, and axes for others to use. Because the citizens at Americus were civilians, Richard Winder could not order them to do the work or provide the materials. But he could—with the permission of the War Department—impress whatever he needed. With this authority, he was able to officially call forth local slaves to do the labor, and construction finally began.

The stockade was a rectangle approximately twice as long as it was wide. The dimensions were approximately 779 feet by 1,400 feet (237 by 427 m), totaling 17 acres (6.7 hectares). The camp was later enlarged and final dimensions were 779 feet by 1,620 feet (494 m) or 27 acres

(11 hectares). The first task was to chop down hundreds of tall pine trees to make the stockade walls. As each tree fell, more sunlight poured into the rectangle. Soon there would be no shade at all. Bonfires of burning pine boughs lit the sky as each day's work continued into the night.

⋅⇥⊨◉⊨⇤⋅

By February 1864, General Winder was desperate to begin the transfer of prisoners from Virginia to Georgia. His urgency was fueled, in part, by rumors of an impending Union raid on Richmond to free the prisoners there. Even though he knew that the Andersonville laborers were still waiting for lumber and nails to construct barracks, Winder ordered the transfer of prisoners to begin. In the Confederate War Department, John B. Jones noted the prisoners' departure in his diary: "We are now sending 400 Federal prisoners to Georgia daily; and I hope we shall have more food in the city when they are gone."

Well-known artist James E. Taylor provided images for *Frank Leslie's Illustrated Newspaper* during the Civil War. Here he imagines what conditions must have been like inside the overcrowded boxcars that carried the Yankee prisoners from Richmond to Andersonville.

The transfer was difficult. Rail was the only way to transport large groups of men, but on many days, trains weren't available. They were needed for other duty—mainly moving troops and supplies. Often an engine broke down or a rail line required repair and this, too, delayed the movement of prisoners. Even when trains were available, moving ten thousand prisoners—hundreds at a time—to the interior of Georgia was a daunting task. No single railroad connected Virginia to Georgia. The route Winder plotted required using nine different rail lines, each with different owners and each requiring separately negotiated fees. Each journey took a week or more, and along the way, prisoners as well as their guards had to be fed.

Meanwhile, Captain Richard Winder appealed to the War Department for shelter at the new prison. If lumber and nails could not be had, then tents would do. The War Department replied that no tents were available. Likewise, the commissary agent assigned to the camp had only a little cornmeal to feed the men—far from adequate to feed the ten thousand men who would arrive shortly. Additionally, the prison's bakehouse was not yet built. And the camp had no baking pans.

In a February 23, 1864, letter, General Winder expressed frustration with the many delays in supplying the new camp at Andersonville. Regarding rations, he wrote that he was willing to compromise by feeding the prisoners "offal" that would not otherwise be sent to Confederate troops. Offal included beef tongue and pickled beef heart. General Winder did not complain about the quality of the offal. He complained about the price he had to pay for it. Two dollars for every beef tongue was simply too expensive. "I shall not want any more," he wrote to the commissary agent.

⟞⟐⟜

In Richmond's Libby Prison, General Dow noted in his diary that February 18, 1864, was another cold night. He feared for the lives of prisoners on Belle Isle. How they must suffer, he wrote. But he also noted that four hundred men had left the island under Confederate guard. They were bound, he learned, for another camp in Americus, Georgia. At least it was warmer there, the general wrote.

Another officer watching from the windows of Libby Prison described the long line of prisoners leaving Belle Isle. The strongest came first. Next came the sick and wounded, leaning on the arms of other soldiers who helped them make the long trek across the bridge. At the end of the line were the near dead. Gaunt and ghost-like, they seemed more like stumbling skeletons than soldiers, the officer wrote. Had he been closer, he might have seen their sunken eyes and cheeks and their dirty and lice-infested clothes. Some were dying from malnutrition and dysentery. Some were feverish, infected with smallpox, a highly contagious and usually deadly disease. Some men would survive their illnesses. Others would not.

The Old Dominion Iron and Nail Works on Belle Isle continued to operate during the war, using Yankee prisoners to supplement their slave labor force. The prisoners crossed the rail bridge, at upper left, when they left Belle Isle for Andersonville.

Ransom wasn't one bit sorry to bid good-bye to Belle Isle. His stay there had been brutal. In January he had tried to escape by jumping into the river. He wasn't shot, the usual fate of escapees, but he was recaptured. His punishment was being bucked and gagged—sitting for hours with arms and legs bound tightly again the chest. That was the bucking part. The gagging was a stick, forced between the teeth and held in place by a string tied behind the ears. That same month, a gang of Union thugs had stolen his boots. Ransom had gone barefoot before managing to purchase another pair of shoes, four sizes too small.

Bucking called for placing a wooden board behind the victim's knees so that they could be pulled closer to his chest.

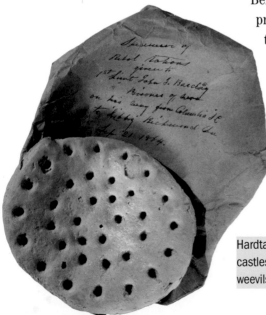

Before leaving Richmond, the Belle Isle prisoners received a ration of hardtack, a type of dry biscuit. In addition, Ransom was able to buy a few boiled potatoes from a guard and to get a pair of woolen socks and new underwear from the U.S. Sanitary Commission. The warm clothing and food fortified him for the cold and cramped conditions of the boxcars in which he was to ride to his new destination.

Hardtack was known as sheet iron crackers, or worm castles, the latter referring to the maggots and weevils that were commonly found in the wafers.

Unlike Ransom—who knew he was going to a different prison camp—prisoner Page was convinced he was going home. He and other hopeful soldiers sang as they marched across the long bridge from Belle Isle to Richmond. One song was about the joyous day when the war would end and all Union soldiers could go home at last:

> *When Johnny comes marching home again,*
> *Hurrah! Hurrah!*
> *We'll give him a hearty welcome then*
> *Hurrah! Hurrah!*
> *The men will cheer and the boys will shout*
> *The ladies they will all turn out,*
> *And we'll all feel gay*
> *When Johnny comes marching home*

Page climbed into the open mouth of a wooden boxcar. The engine hissed and sparked and finally chugged forward. The train crossed the James River, passing Belle Isle. Although the rails ran south toward Petersburg, Virginia, on the coast, Page wasn't worried. Surely a ship flying a flag of truce would be waiting there to accept the prisoners on exchange. By morning, however, Page's hopes had begun to fade. They were still traveling south.

The trains navigated a slow and rumbling route: from Richmond to Petersburg, then onward to Gordonsville, Virginia. Here the guards ordered the prisoners out of the cars to camp the night on the ground between rail lines. At Danville the train stopped, and again the guards ordered the prisoners out. They marched to another rail line and another string of dilapidated boxcars that smelled of cattle and dung.

Many a soldier believed the cars might lurch off the tracks, so rough was the track bed over which they traveled. "Destitution stares Virginia in the face," one prisoner wrote, noting the ruined fields and burned plantations from the train that passed slowly by.

In some cars, the men had no room to lie down. The train slowed to a crawl and then stopped altogether for hours on a side track to allow another train to pass. Then the engine sputtered forward again, wood smoke trailing behind in a dark ribbon. The rattling journey continued southward to Gaston, North Carolina, and then Raleigh. Along the way, the trains stopped frequently and the prisoners waited—for wood to be loaded to fuel the engine, for another train to pass, or for other reasons neither the prisoners nor their guards could figure out.

Along the way, the prisoners received military rations of crackers, bacon, and cornmeal. But on some days, the mule-drawn wagons with that day's rations never came. A soldier from Pennsylvania recalled having only peanuts to eat for an entire day.

At a stop in Charlotte, North Carolina, women milled around the rails with baskets of goods—a dozen ginger cookies, a sweet potato pie—to sell to prisoners who had money. The local citizens needed the money, and so the Confederate guards looked the other way, allowing the transactions to take place, though they were not encouraged. Some days, rain drizzled. Other days the sun steamed, turning the boxcars into sweatboxes. At night the men slept sitting up in the boxcars, scratching at lice in their hair and on their arms and legs. Some nights, the guard ordered the men out of the cars into the dark. Often the ground alongside the track was their bed. On those nights, the guards took aim at anyone who stood up to walk about. More than one bluecoat lost his life by not heeding the warning.

Where to? the men asked themselves as the cars pulled away from Columbia, South Carolina. Charleston, suggested some who remembered their schoolbook geography. Savannah, suggested others. But the train veered westward toward the interior of Georgia and away from these coastal cities. During a stop in Augusta, Georgia, a Southern woman offered prisoner Charles Hopkins a piece of cake and some milk. Her son was a Confederate soldier, she explained. She hoped someone in the North would treat him as kindly.

Macon, Georgia, was the end of the line for the commissioned officers aboard the train. The city's fairgrounds was the site of a prisoner-of-war camp for Union officers. The citizens of Macon weren't any happier than the citizens of Andersonville to host a camp for Richmond's bluecoats, even if they were officers. As early as 1862, a writer for the *Macon Daily Telegraph* complained that there wasn't food enough to feed both the citizens of Macon and the Yankees. "We have no place to hold them—no food to give them—nobody whose time can be well spared to guard them." Housing prisoners of war cost money, as much as one thousand dollars a day, the newspaper writer estimated. That was "a good deal more than [paying for] . . . the same number of effective troops in the field."

The trains continued on with the enlisted men. At last, they realized that they, too, were bound for a prison camp, not an exchange. And now the name of the place was spoken: Camp Sumter at Anderson Station, the guards said. The guards on later trains would simply say "Andersonville."

Camp Oglethorpe opened in Macon, Georgia, in 1862 to house Union officers. It became known among prisoners for the number of escape tunnel operations beneath the enclosure.

What kind of a place is it? the men wanted to know. One Union prisoner remembered the pleasant description the guard gave to him: the camp was a fenced pen with grassy hillsides surrounded by pine trees and plenty of fresh air. "Too good for you Yanks anyway," the guard said.

⟶══◎◎══⟵

About 60 miles (97 km) of rail linked Macon with Anderson Station. On this final leg of the journey, the train moved no faster than a man could run. Union prisoner John McElroy stared at the passing landscape: a forest of tall pines, flat stretches of sandy banks, and an occasional muddy swamp. He was certain that nothing worth eating could grow out of the iron red Georgia soil.

McElroy was seventeen. He had been a soldier for less than a year, volunteering for the 16th Illinois Calvary. Like so many others, he had been captured during a surprise attack and sent to Richmond's prisons. He, too, was among the bluecoats packed into boxcars bound for Andersonville.

Near midnight on the seventh day of McElroy's journey—or was it the eighth or ninth, time moved so slowly—the locomotive hissed and the cars jolted to a stop at Anderson Station. The guard ordered the men out of the cars. They moved slowly, stiff-legged from days in the crowded boxes. Some could not climb down to the small platform and

The early prisoners were not impressed with their crude new quarters at Andersonville. But they could not even imagine how much worse it was going to get as an endless stream of men poured into the enclosure.

required the help of others. Outside the cars, most took a deep breath of fresh air. The night was thick with the smell of pine. A dirt road led away from the rail line into the pitch-dark forest. Guards stood along both sides of the dirt road, lit with flaming torches of pine knots. A quarter of a mile (0.4 km) down the road, the prisoners came to a great wall of squared pine logs standing upright in the ground, rising 15 feet (4.6 m) high. A pair of massive wooden gates hung from the palisade (fence) with iron hinges. As the prisoners watched, the wide gates slowly began to open. Beyond, in an open space stripped of trees, lay the camp. It was "a hole cut in this wilderness," McElroy wrote.

"A dismal hole," Ransom would later write in his diary.

This, then, was the end of the line.

A CONFEDERATE PRISONER TRANSPORT

Seriously wounded in the Battle of Malvern Hill, Virginia, in June 1862, Anthony Keiley returned to his home in Petersburg, Virginia. There, he served the Confederacy as a home guard. In June 1864, while defending his town from a Yankee skirmish, Keiley was captured. The Union soldiers force-marched Keiley and their other prisoners 26 miles (42 km) to the Virginia coast. Here the captives boarded the U.S. ship *John Warren* for the journey to a prison in the North. The guard ordered the rebel prisoners below deck into stables that had once been used to transport cavalry horses. More "intolerable" to the Confederate prisoners than the stables, however, was their Union guard—a regiment of African American soldiers. Southerners did not like the idea of being under the watch of people they considered to be inferior to whites.

The first stop on Keiley's journey north was Point Lookout Prison on a spit of land on the Maryland shore between the Potomac River and the Chesapeake Bay. Tents provided shelter. For many Confederate prisoners, Point Lookout was simply a holding pen until the next ship arrived to transport them farther north. And so it was for Keiley. After three weeks, he boarded *El Cid*, bound for New York City. He spent the two-day sea voyage sweltering below deck.

Once docked in the harbor, the prisoners were marched through the streets to a train station and onto boxcars. The locomotive's whistle screamed as the train pulled away from the depot. The destination was Elmira, a city in western New York State. Keiley was an educated man and

Confederate prisoners are lined up outside their barracks at Elmira prison in about 1864. Close to one quarter of the more than twelve thousand Confederate soldiers imprisoned at Elmira died there. Seventeen escaped.

understood that this remote location was, for at least four months of the year, a frigid, snow-covered wilderness.

At Elmira the prisoners were marched double column from the train depot to the prison stockade. Inside the palisade were thirty barracks, hastily built by the Union to accommodate the growing number of Confederate prisoners of war. On July 12, 1864, Keiley became prisoner 766. In the months to come, the number of prisoners would overcrowd the barracks. The snows of winter and the inadequately heated barracks would not be the only hardship Keiley would face. Reduced rations and the spread of disease would cause the death of thousands of his fellow prisoners. Keiley was among those who would survive and later write a book about his imprisonment.

CHAPTER THREE
THE FLYING DUTCHMAN

[Wirz] is a lean, tall, rough, coarse-looking German. He swears incessantly and curses most cruelly. . . . A cold chill ran over me when I thought he was to have command and control of our men.

—CHAPLAIN HENRY S. WHITE,
PRISON LIFE AMONG THE REBELS, 1864

On February 27, 1864, James Madison Page walked through the gates of Andersonville. He joined approximately two thousand other prisoners of war who had arrived a few days earlier. One wall of the palisade was not yet complete. A crew of more than a hundred African American slaves was still digging the palisade trench into which the logs would be placed in an upright position. rebel soldiers defended this breach in the stockade so no bluecoats could escape.

Before the war, Page had worked as a surveyor, measuring land to determine boundaries and elevations. He viewed the camp with the same scientific eye and noted that inside the pen were felled logs and brush, material the prisoners could use to build shelters. He gathered the boys from his Michigan regiment. The eleven from Belle Isle were now ten—one man had died on the train to Americus. They chose a site at the south end of the camp, about 12 feet (3.6 m) from the fence

itself. They used the limbs and boughs from the cast-aside pine trees to build a sort of shanty with a shady roof in front. Page felt fortunate. He had reasonable shelter, and while the ration of beans and bacon was not particularly tasty and the cornmeal was coarse, he at least had food enough for the moment.

Within days, the first prisoners of Andersonville had settled in. Like Page and the men of the Michigan regiment, they built huts, called shebangs, with pine poles and boughs. They dug up vines and roots from the bog along the creek and wove them into thatch roofs to provide some shade. Others used their blankets or their overcoats to fashion crude tents.

A. J. Riddle, a Confederate photographer from nearby Macon, Georgia, was able to take a number of photographs depicting conditions in Andersonville. Here he shows the crude tents constructed by the early arrivals at Andersonville. The men who came later would find that all the available materials had been taken, so they would have to get by with no shelter.

By March the final wall of the stockade had been erected. The only way in or out of the pen was through one of two gates. The north gate was on one side of the stream. On the other side of the stream was the south gate. Twice each day, the south gate opened and a mule-drawn wagon entered. It carried the morning and the afternoon rations. The prisoners each received 1 quart (1 liter) of cornmeal, a sweet potato, and a few ounces of salt beef. Prisoners scavenged pine knots from the ground to make a small, sooty fire over which to cook their food. For water, they waded through the bog on either side of the stream, legs sinking knee deep in the muck. The camp had no dishes, so the men improvised. A hat, a knotted shirtsleeve, or a boot—all would serve in the coming months as containers for gathering water and mixing the cornmeal into a dough that could be fried on a piece of tin from a canteen.

A Confederate officer, Lieutenant Colonel Alexander Persons, was the commander of the interior of the stockade where the prisoners lived and of the military camp along the stream above the stockade where the guards lived. Persons was lenient with the prisoners. He allowed small groups to go outside the pen to gather wood and additional pine boughs for fuel and shelter. In mid-March, however, rumors began to circulate that a new commandant would replace Persons. Rumors started easily and spread quickly inside Andersonville. Page wrote, "No statement, no matter how weird, wonderful, improbable, wild or incredible, once started in the prison, would not have its couriers [messengers] . . . and its believers." The rumor about the new commandant was that he was a German who spoke with an accent and who hated all Yankees. The rumors were close to true.

⋆⇀⟹⟸↼⋆

Two months earlier, on January 20, 1864, the Confederate ship *A. D. Vance* had steamed into North Carolina's Wilmington harbor.

The 902-ton (818-metric-ton) iron, side-wheel ship was one of the fastest and most successful blockade-runners on the ocean. At night, when dark clouds obscured the black steam from her twin stacks, she would steal out of port, carrying cotton bound for Europe. Among the passengers on this particular return voyage from Europe was Captain Henry Wirz.

Wirz was on leave from the Confederate army due to an injury. He claimed to have been wounded in the Battle of Seven Pines at Henrico County, Virginia, on May 31, 1862. Two bullets, known as minié balls, fired from a Union soldier's musket had crushed the bones in his right forearm and wrist. His promotion from lieutenant to captain came twelve days after that battle, suggesting that the Confederacy had rewarded his bravery. Some historians, however, believe Wirz made up the story of his injury. Some accounts suggest Wirz's injury was the result of a stagecoach accident. Either way—through courage in battle or simply a twist of fate—the shattered wrist did not completely heal. In addition, nerve damage had paralyzed his ring and little fingers. The injury permanently disabled him.

Why Wirz had traveled to Europe was also unknown. His daughter would later claim that Confederate president

While in Paris, France, Wirz posed for a formal photograph wearing his uniform. His officer's sash is tied over the shoulder and knotted at the waist. The pose successfully masked any injury to his arm he might have suffered

Davis had sent him to Europe on a diplomatic mission. No official records document such an assignment. While in Europe, Wirz had sought treatment for his injury in Paris, France. A surgeon there had removed dead tissue and bone chips from the officer's forearm. The wound seemed to be healing, although Wirz's two fingers remained paralyzed. After the operation, Wirz traveled to Switzerland, the country of his birth, where he spent three months recuperating. From Switzerland, he traveled to the United Kingdom and booked passage back to the United States on the *A. D. Vance*. While at sea, his wound reopened and infection inflamed his arm.

Wirz was forty years old when he returned to Wilmington, North Carolina, in January, 1864. He was of medium build, his hair was just beginning to gray, and he wore a black beard, cropped short. A long

Artist James E. Taylor drawing for *Frank Leslie's Illustrated Newspaper* shows Captain Wirz straightening a line of prisoners. Some historians think that Taylor obtained access to Andersonville by agreeing to do favorable drawings of Wirz at work but, once inside, took advantage of the opportunity to depict the true conditions there.

scar crossed his left shoulder. The deltoid muscle was so weakened that raising his left arm caused grimacing pain, and he often stood with his shoulders hunched. Wirz was no longer able to shoulder a musket or lunge with a bayonet.

Wirz had previously served as a commander of a Confederate prisoner-of-war camp in Tuscaloosa, Alabama. He had also served on General Winder's staff in Richmond, assisting in managing the city's prisons, including Belle Isle. In February 1864, as boxcars of blue-coats rolled toward Anderson Station, Wirz once again reported for duty to General Winder. The general assigned Wirz to Andersonville, where he reported to Persons.

Wirz arrived at Andersonville about March 25, 1864. Wirz's job was to enforce prisoner discipline inside the pen and to ensure that no one escaped. He did not have command over the military camp or the soldiers outside the pen. And although he was not responsible for securing or distributing food, he could withhold rations as punishment.

A full week passed before Wirz stepped inside the stockade to review his prisoners. When he did, the prisoners discovered that Wirz had been a foreigner. Born in Switzerland, he had moved to the United States in 1849 and had become a U.S. citizen. His native language was German. He also spoke Dutch and English fluently, although his English was accented. Before the war, he had been an apprentice to a doctor and later worked as a doctor in a small Louisiana town. But Wirz had no medical degree from any university. He struggled to make a living for his wife and children. When the war began, he had enlisted as a private in the Confederate army.

Both Ransom and McElroy recorded their first impressions of the new commandant in their diaries. Ransom wrote, "[Wirz] came inside today and looked us over. Is not a very prepossessing [impressive] looking chap. . . skin has a pale, white livered look, with thin lips.

PRISON SLANG

Doodledom: a term some Confederate prisoners of war used to refer to the North

flanker: a thief

fresh fish: newly arrived prisoners

Galvanized Yankees: Union prisoners of war or deserters from the army who enlisted in the Confederate army

God's Country: a term some Union prisoners of war used to refer to the North

hen buttons: the eagle on the buttons of Union uniforms. Union prisoners sold or traded these buttons for food or other goods from Confederate prison guards. (The eagle is the national bird of the United States.)

shebang: shelters, based on the Irish word *shebeen*, which generally refers to an illegal place to serve alcohol

skedaddle: to run away

swallowing the eagle: a phrase to describe Confederate prisoners of war who pledged allegiance to the United States. In return, they were allowed amnesty (pardon) but had to remain in the North for the duration of the war.

Has a sneering sort of cast of countenance [look]. Makes a fellow feel as if he would like to go up and boot him." McElroy first saw Wirz during a morning roll call. "He was an undersized, fidgety man," he wrote, "with an insignificant face and a mouth that protruded like a rabbit's." He compared Wirz's eyes to a rat's. And rats, McElroy noted, were cunning creatures who survived by stealing from others.

Wirz was forming his first impressions as well. With his previous experience managing prisons, he understood that this assignment would be unpleasant. Even so, the despicable conditions at Andersonville greatly distressed him. The cookhouse was still not complete. The camp had no nails, axes, buckets, or shovels. Quartermaster Captain Richard Winder had somehow secured thirty-five tents to serve as the camp hospital. But set inside the stockade (as a way of preventing patients' escape), the hospital's location endangered healthy prisoners. Even worse, the tents had been pitched near the camp's latrines, or toilets, known as sinks. The foul matter in the stagnant water endangered everyone.

Unsanitary conditions were everywhere. Wirz saw that the guard campsite was on the creek above the stockade. The guards bathed

Photographer A. J. Riddle of Macon, Georgia, shot this elevated view of Andersonville during his visit to the camp on August 17, 1864.

in this creek and also used it for their toilet. This dirty water then flowed into the stockade for the use of the prisoners. The stream that had been clear and swift when Page entered Andersonville in February was polluted by the time Wirz arrived a month later. Once the bakehouse was completed on the creek above the stockade, Wirz noted that the cooks tossed garbage and refuse into the water. A greasy green slime collected on the surface and this, too, flowed into the stockade. With no sanitation policy at the camp, the guards did not enter the stockade to clear away the filth, and the prisoners themselves seemed uninterested in doing so. Additionally, Wirz worried about the inexperience of the camp's guards. Even when the stockade walls were completed, prisoners managed to slip away from the guards in broad daylight as they were scavenging wood outside the stockade. Most were quickly recaptured by the camp's hound dogs, but the problem persisted.

⋄⇒◯◌⇐⋄

Wirz had come to Georgia with his wife and daughters. They rented rooms in a home owned by a local resident about 2 miles (3 km) from camp. Wirz forbade his family from coming near the stockade. Early each morning, Wirz left his home and reported for duty. He did not dress in a Confederate uniform. Instead, he wore a white linen shirt and light-colored pants and black leather boots. Buckled around his waist was a holster and in it, a revolver. He did not hesitate to remove it and wave it at the prisoners, shouting at them to fall in line.

His headquarters was a shack, quickly hammered together on a small hill above the stockade. A pine board sign announced his name and title: Captain Wirz, Commander of the Inner Prison. From his headquarters, Wirz could see both gates of the stockade. He could also see the railroad tracks and observe the movement of guards and of prisoners who had permission to work outside the pen.

DISTRIBUTION OF RATIONS

At three or four o'clock each afternoon, Andersonville's stockade gate opened. A driver snapped the reins over the backs of a team of tired mules drawing a wagonload of rations. The prisoners crowded forward to get a better look, even though the fare was always the same: bacon and cornmeal, sometimes rice and molasses. The sergeants for each prisoner squad received the rations and then divided them among the men. Before the completion of the bakehouse, the men received their rations raw. Cooking was their responsibility. Once the bakehouse began operations, its ovens could not keep up. And so, on alternate days, half the camp received cooked corn bread while the other half received raw meal. When a man had firewood, he fixed his bacon onto a stick and toasted it over the flame. Other days, he simply ate it raw.

The men mixed their cornmeal with water to make mush or dough that could be rolled into dumplings. Rations rarely included salt. To spice up the bland mush or dumplings, McElroy bartered with the guards for peppers and mixed them into the cornmeal. Men often shared their rations, cooking larger portions over a single fire to save wood. One prisoner described his half-cooked ration of beef and rice as so sour as to "vomit a Hog." Another compared his baked corn bread to fruitcake—except flies took the place of raisins.

Wirz knew that the food was of poor quality and a cause of sickness inside the stockade. On June 3, 1864, he wrote to a superior officer about the problem. "I most respectfully call the attention of the colonel . . . to the following facts: The bread which is issued to prisoners is of such an inferior quality, consisting fully of one-sixth of husk, that it is almost unfit for use and increasing dysentery and other bowel complaints."

Despite Wirz's report, nothing changed.

Soon after Wirz took command of the interior of Andersonville, an order came from Richmond to reduce the prisoners' rations. The decision was not Wirz's, but the men inside the pen did not know this. All they knew was that soon after Wirz arrived, they got less to eat. And they blamed him for it.

Wirz was responsible, however, for the construction of the deadline. Soldiers understood the purpose of a deadline—to control the movement of prisoners so they could not overpower the guards or escape. To build the deadline, workers drove stakes into the ground inside the pen and hammered together a railing. This interior "fence" was 15 feet (4.6 m) from the stockade walls and encircled the entire pen. The guards threatened to shoot—and began to do so—anyone who ventured under or beyond the rail. Even extending a hand across the deadline, reaching for a fallen bit of food, could mean a bullet in the head. Many prisoners believed Wirz had promised each guard a furlough of thirty days if he shot and killed a Yankee prisoner.

A Union prisoner is shot by a guard for reaching across the deadline. The prisoners in line behind him hold crude containers to collect water for which they were so desperate.

William Waud, English-born architect and illustrator, sketched a new batch of "fresh fish" arriving at Andersonville sometime between February 1864 and April 1865. Like James E. Taylor, he worked for *Frank Leslie's Illustrated Newspaper*.

In the early weeks of his command, Wirz frequently left his headquarters and entered the stockade. Accompanied by guards, he walked through the camp searching for signs of escape tunnels. Prisoners sometimes approached him. They asked to be allowed to go outside the pen to cut wood. Others asked for soap or for wheat bread to eat instead of the coarse cornmeal that cramped their stomachs and loosened their bowels. In his diary, Ransom recorded the comment Wirz frequently used in reply to those requests for better food: "It is good enough for you Yankees."

Each train that arrived at Andersonville brought hundreds of "fresh fish," the term the men inside the pen used for new prisoners. Wirz met the trains. He rode a white mare, spurring the horse up and down the line. As each boxcar emptied, Wirz ordered the men into groups of ninety. He cursed if they did not fall in line quickly enough to please him. He threatened to set the dogs on them should they attempt to escape.

Like Belle Isle, Andersonville was a camp for enlisted men. The highest-ranking officers were sergeants. Wirz ordered the sergeants to step forward. Those who could write recorded the names of the men within each ninety. Each morning at roll call, these nineties would fall in line, and if all men were accounted for, they would then receive their rations.

If someone was missing, the captain warned, the entire group would go without food that day. This was Wirz's way of keeping track of the growing population inside the pen. It was also a means to discourage escape.

By the time T. H. Mann arrived in May 1863, more than thirteen thousand prisoners were crammed inside a prison originally built to house ten thousand. He unfolded his stiff legs and climbed out of the boxcar in which he had been riding. He noticed a spiral of black smoke curling upward in the distance. "That's where you Yanks will be put up," a guard said. "Fall in, you darn Yankee sons of bitches," Wirz ordered. He rode his horse to the head of the line and ordered the prisoners to march forward behind him. Upon reaching the gates, the line halted. The gates swung open to reveal another set of doors. These interior gates opened only after the gates behind the new prisoners had shut and the guards had heavily barred them. T. H. Mann watched as these inner gates now opened.

"Fresh fish! Fresh fish!" the cry went up from inside.

The guards ushered the new prisoners forward.

"Our hearts sickened as we first looked upon the misery before our eyes," Mann would later write. To Mann, the prisoners seemed half human, half ghost.

The human ghosts crowded around the newcomers. They clamored for news—news of the war, of home, and of exchange. Always there was the hope of exchange.

"Look out for the deadline!" they warned.

Warren Lee Goss of Maine arrived at Andersonville on May 1, 1864. The rain was falling hard and cold that day. He was miserable from days in the bumping, rocking boxcars. The "ferocious, round-shouldered little man" on the bay mare who cursed and sputtered at Goss's regiment struck the soldier as "ridiculous." He and others among his regiment began to laugh at the commandant. "By Got! You Tam

Yankees!" Wirz shouted in his German-accented English. "You won't laugh ven you get inside the bull pen."

What Wirz said was true. When the stockade gates swung open, Goss got his first sight of true misery. The filthy men swarming around him were so begrimed with pine smoke that he could not be certain if they were white men or black men. Their tattered uniforms were faded to grimy grey. Many wore no shirts at all, no shoes, and no caps to shield them from the downpour. Men lay on the ground half naked, covered with lice, sick and weak, and dying from neglect. Goss swallowed his laughter.

As newcomers, Mann and Goss were shocked by the reduced condition of what had once been a proud, healthy army of soldiers. Even those such as Ransom, Page, and McElroy—who had been inside the pen for three months—still shuddered at the suffering and the dying.

T. Sinclair, a well-known Philadelphia lithographer, based his 1864 north view of Andersonville on a sketch by John B. Walker, an imprisoned private from a Pennsylvania unit.

"Our government must hear of our condition here and get us away before long," Ransom wrote in his diary. "If they don't, it's a poor government to tie to."

⊶═◉═⊷

On May 8, 1864, six weeks after taking command of the interior of the camp, Wirz wrote his first report to his superior officer. "I found the camp in a bad condition owing to the want of tools, such as axes, spades, and lumber to erect proper buildings." He commented on the poorly situated hospital and noted an urgent need for additional guards to prevent a mass escape. And he wrote about the overcrowding: "The necessity of enlarging the stockade is unavoidable and I will commence as soon as I can gather a sufficient number of Negroes."

The final paragraph of his report was about himself. "I am in a very unpleasant position, growing out of the rank that I now hold," he wrote. As captain, he held no authority over the other officers. As a result, his orders were not often obeyed. "My duties are manifold [many] and required all my time in daytime and very often part of the night." He asked for a promotion.

In Richmond, General Winder read Wirz's report. He added a comment to the document. Wirz was "a diligent and efficient officer," the general wrote. Despite the general's vote of confidence in the commandant, the Confederate War Department did not promote Wirz.

That same month, two officers arrived at Andersonville from Richmond to inspect the camp. They had come under General Winder's orders. In his report, Captain Walter Bowie noted that one-fourth of the land was "wet and marshy and in its present condition altogether unfit for an encampment." Bowie had confidence that Wirz would complete a project within a few weeks to drain the wetland and dam the stream at two points, using the higher level for drinking water and the lower for bathing. Bowie ended his report by praising Wirz's "zeal" in fulfilling his duties.

Maine private Thomas O'Dea drew Andersonville as it appeared on August, 1, 1864, when the structure contained thirty-five thousand Union prisoners.

The second officer was Major Thomas Turner. He, too, noted the wretched conditions in camp. Much work was needed, he stated, to make the camp habitable. He believed Wirz would improve the camp's interior but only if he had help. Turner recommended at least two commissioned officers be assigned under Wirz. His report concluded: "Captain Wirz . . . in my opinion deserves great credit for the good sense and energy he has displayed in the management of the prison at Andersonville. He is the only man who seems to fully comprehend his important duties. He does the work of commandant, adjutant, clerk, and warden, and without his presence . . . everything would be chaos and confusion."

Again, General Winder endorsed the reports. And again, the Confederate War Department refused to promote Wirz and assign him additional officers. Clearly the War Department's priorities were the Confederate troops in the field and not the Union prisoners in the pen.

A LETTER TO JEFFERSON DAVIS

Deadlines were common in prisoner-of-war camps, both in the North and in the South. In Elmira, New York, the prison camp had an "invisible" deadline. Confederate prisoners understood that they could go no closer than 15 feet (4.6 m) from the prison wall for fear of being shot. In Andersonville, the line was clearly visible, a narrow post and rail border.

James E. Anderson, a soldier in the First Georgia Reserves assigned to guarding the Andersonville stockade, was disturbed by the number of prisoners who were shot at the deadline. Although he was a lowly private, Anderson felt compelled to bring the matter to the attention of Jefferson Davis, the president of the Confederacy.

> *Inside our prison walls all around there is a space about twelve feet [3.7 m] wide, called the "dead-line." If a prisoner crosses that line the sentinels [guards] are ordered to shoot him. Now, we have many thoughtless boys here who think the killing of a Yankee will make them great men. As a consequence, every day or two there are prisoners shot. . . . The*

Inside Andersonville, the prisoners gave one another nicknames: Big Charlie, Little Jim, Skinny, and Smarty. One prisoner earned the name Romeo because of his ability to quote lines from William Shakespeare's plays. The men gave Wirz a name too, the Flying Dutchman. Most likely the name was a reference to Wirz's foreignness, his German accent. But some in the camp may have known the legend of the Flying Dutchman, an old folktale about a ship's headstrong captain *sentry, of course, says he was across the deadline when he shot him. He is told he did exactly right and is a good sentry. . . . Night before last there was one shot near me (I being on guard). The sentry said that the Yankee made one step across the line to avoid a mud hole. He shot him through the bowels, and when the officer of the guard got there he was lying inside their own lines. He (the sentry) as usual told him that he stepped across, but fell back inside. The officer told him it was exactly right. Now, my dear sir, I know you are opposed to such measures, and I make this statement to you knowing you to be a soldier, statesman, and Christian, that if possible you may correct such things, together with many others that exist here . . . but let a good man come here as a private citizen and mix with the privates and stay one week, and if he don't find out things revolting to humanity then I am deceived. I shall put my name to this, believing that you will not let the officers over me see it, otherwise I would suffer, most probably.*

PRIVATE JAMES E. ANDERSON

and his crew, doomed to sail the ocean forever. In one version, the captain is too stubborn to turn sail in the face of a storm. In another version, the captain allows a terrible crime to occur aboard ship. Afterward, no port will allow the crew to come ashore. In both versions, the Flying Dutchman is a ghost ship.

In the legend, the captain, too, is trapped aboard his doomed ship. Wirz had been commander of Andersonville for less than two months, but already he—like the legendary captain—was becoming its prisoner.

CHAPTER FOUR
THE WILL TO SURVIVE

*The rations were miserable and wholly inadequate . . .
two buckets of mush for ninety men. "Chicken feed," the
boys called it and it seemed a very appropriate name,
for it was nothing but coarse corn meal and water with a
little salt, half cooked.*
—ROBERT KELLOGG, *LIFE AND DEATH IN REBEL PRISONS*, 1867

Daily life in Andersonville followed a monotonous pattern. Early each morning, a drumbeat signaled roll call. The prisoners gathered into their squads of ninety. Those too sick to walk crawled to the line or a comrade carried them. The rebel sergeant in charge of roll call tallied the number of prisoners, striking out the names of anyone who had died during the night. The sergeant then reported these numbers to Wirz. The commandant, in turn, requisitioned the day's rations.

Each man followed his own routine. Ransom bathed himself daily. Then he walked around the camp to visit friends and inquire after their health. He walked past the gates, where the corpses were stacked, looking to see if anyone he knew had died during the night. In the early weeks, the number of bodies each day had been few. By June 1864, however, the number of deaths each day had increased to more than one hundred a day.

About ten in the morning, sick call began. Hundreds gathered at the south gate. In early June 1864, Andersonville had only thirteen Confederate doctors, not nearly enough to care for a prison population that had risen by this time to more than twenty-six thousand. The doctors had few medicines to distribute to the sick. Nor did they have beds and blankets for all who needed them. As a result, the doctors admitted only the most critical cases to the hospital.

Private John Ransom included this overview of Andersonville in his diary. Note the hospital tents under the trees at top of drawing.

BURYING THE DEAD

When a prisoner died at Andersonville, those in his squad held a simple funeral service. They gathered to share a few solemn moments and good memories. Many prayed. They distributed the dead man's possessions among themselves. Often the possessions were just a shirt or a cap or a pair of boots, a spoon, a plate, or a book. Still, such things provided comfort to the living. Very often, prior to dying, a man might press the photograph of his wife or mother into the hand of a comrade and ask him to return it to the woman so loved. Vows were given to do just that. These vows comforted many in their final hours.

To prepare the body for burial, the men tied the two big toes of the dead person together. Then they wrote the man's name and his regiment on a piece of paper and tagged it to the toes. They folded his hands over his chest and carried him to the gate. They laid him on the ground and turned away. The charnel wagon (a wagon for transporting dead bodies) came once a day, usually in the morning, to remove the bodies from inside the stockade.

Early on there had been scrap lumber for coffins. But soon there was none. Outside the stockade, Wirz had assigned prisoners to dig trenches for the mass burial of the dead. They generally stripped the dead of whatever clothing remained. Then they placed the bodies one alongside another, often with bony shoulders and knees touching. The names of the dead were recorded by a clerk in a ledger kept in Wirz's headquarters.

Photographer A. J. Riddle used his camera to record the horrors of Andersonville during his visit to the camp on August 17, 1864. Here dead prisoners are being lowered into burial trenches.

For this reason, nursing sick friends was a daily reality for prisoners inside the stockade. The healthy carried water for the sick in their squads. They fed those too weak to cook their own meals.

The camp hospital was in a grove of trees on the southeastern corner outside the stockade. Approximately 5 acres (2 hectares) in size, the space was enclosed by a pine log fence similar to that surrounding the prison pen. Here were tents to shelter the patients. Rather than corn bread, which the physicians agreed made the men's diarrhea worse, the rations included rice. As in the stockade, mosquitoes and flies swarmed. Maggots crawled in gangrenous wounds. Here, too, the men lay in their lice-infested clothing, tattooed still from the pine smoke from the interior of the stockade. Most of the "nurses" were prisoners who were allowed to assist the hospital's few doctors. More than a few of those nurses had robbed the sick of their blankets and then sold them to the guards.

Isaiah H. White, the surgeon in charge of the prisoners' hospital at Andersonville, wrote letters to the Confederate War Department. Soon after he reported for duty, he complained about the size of the stockade and the overcrowding that endangered the men's health. In May and then again in June, he wrote reports to the Confederate War Department, noting the lack of doctors at Andersonville. The sick were without tents, beds, and even straw to spread on the ground for a bed. More often than not, White had no medicines for treating the imprisoned patients.

Although the hospital was outside the stockade, few prisoners wanted to go there. The patients admitted to the hospital rarely recovered. The secret to survival, the prisoners believed, was staying out of the hospital at all costs. That meant not only taking care of your own needs for food and shelter but relying on the help of others.

The will to survive was strong at Andersonville. And to survive meant drinking and eating. But how could a man drink if the stream was fouled with human waste? How could he eat if the cornmeal issued to him was raw and he had no firewood and pan in which to fry it?

Staying alive also meant staying clean. But how could a man clean himself when he had no soap to scrub away the pine smoke? And even if a piece of soap were to come his way, the camp water was filthy. Staying alive meant being sheltered from the sun and rain and cold dews. But how could a man shelter himself without a tent or a blanket? Or clothe himself once pants and shirts and shoes had worn out?

The prisoners solved these problems in various and often creative ways. Before the war, most prisoners had not been soldiers. They had worked as tradesmen or farmers. Some were blacksmiths or watchmakers. There were dentists and cobblers. Inside the stockade, the men tapped their talents and put them to use. A barber cut the long, matted hair of the prisoners who had the coins to pay for that service. A soldier from Illinois managed to use an old iron hoop to fashion a saw and pocket knife. With these sharp-edged tools, he carved buckets out of scraps of wood, which he got by bartering with the guards. He could make one bucket a day and sold each for a dollar. A bucket was a valuable possession for it meant a man could carry water to any part of the camp. He could receive his rations in a bucket or use it as a bowl to mix mush.

Prisoners dug wells for freshwater. On the north side, the soil had high clay content. In some places, the men had only to dig a few feet to reach the water table. The water that bubbled up was muddy and gritty but generally cooler and cleaner than the sluggish stream. The men foraged for fuel, digging in the stinking swamp near the creek for pine roots that would burn when dried. Some men shaped mud into

Despite the overcrowding and lack of sanitation, life in Andersonville went on. The prisoners established their own rules for commerce and punishment. This view of stockade life as seen from the main gate was published in *Harper's Weekly* in 1866, a time when Northerners were being told the details of what had gone on there.

bricks, let the sun bake them, and then used those bricks to build ovens. In these ovens, they baked cornmeal into small loaves and sold them. Others went into business selling cups of soup made from foraged ingredients.

Prisoners mended clothing using thread unraveled from a meal sack or a sock. When it rained, men removed their clothing and allowed nature to wash not only their tattered pants and shirts but also their naked bodies. Ransom went into the laundry business with a Native American from Minnesota called Battese. Battese showed Ransom how to make a washboard by carving ridges on the surface of a piece of scrap lumber. Battese and Ransom had no soap, but water and sand and hard scrubbing removed some of the pine smoke and sweat from the clothing. Ransom made a shingle on which he printed *WASHING* and set it in front of his shebang. If a prisoner had no money, then Ransom accepted bread in exchange for his services. He estimated that he could earn 1 pound (0.45 kg) of bread for a day or two of work.

LICE

While assigned to the Andersonville prison, the Confederate physician Dr. John Bates learned the practical meaning of the term *lousy*. "Of vermin and lice," he stated, "there was a very prolific crop. . . . I would generally find some upon myself after retiring to my quarters. They were so numerous that it was impossible for a surgeon to enter the hospital without having some upon him when he came out."

"Lousy" describes a person infested with body lice. These small, wingless insects tormented the men both inside and outside the stockade at Andersonville. But the men inside the stockade suffered especially, for the sandy ground was infested with the insects. John McElroy compared the lice that climbed up his legs to "streams of ants swarming up a tree."

The insect is gray or brown, has six legs, and mouthparts that enable it to pierce the skin of its human host. The louse feeds on blood. The bites of the louse produce an itch that can become infected if the host scratches the bites to the point of irritation.

A female louse may lay as many as two to three hundred eggs during her brief lifetime. Generally, she lays the eggs in the host's clothing, most often in the seams or creases of fabric.

Frequent bathing and frequent washing of clothing in very hot water kills lice. But the men in Andersonville had neither soap nor firewood nor kettles to boil water to wash their clothing. The best they could do was to remove their clothing, then hold the fabric over a flame, causing the louse eggs to burst.

The daily skirmish with lice took hours. Often they worked in teams, each man delousing the other, picking the nits, or insect eggs, from his matted hair and beards. Men too weak or sick to perform this ritual were soon literally crawling with lice.

For shelter, men pitched in together to dig small caves in the north hillside or to burrow into the ground. They shared blankets and overcoats, using them for roofs during the day to create shade. At night the same blanket or overcoat became a mattress, offering a little protection from the cool, damp ground. Summer in Andersonville was brutal. Sun blistered the skin. Men burrowed into hillside holes to escape the glare and also the mosquitoes. The swampy acres on either side of the creek bred swarms of them. The insects fed on the men, leaving bloody welts that rose along their arms and legs, backs and face. So many were the bites, reported one Confederate medical officer, that the men appeared to be suffering from the measles. Given the men's weakened conditions, the bites often became infected.

A society with neighborhoods soon developed within the stockade. As in any society, some neighborhoods were more favorable than others. Pitching a shebang near the bog that bordered the contaminated stream was less desirable than a location on the north hillside. A site with a well was quite valuable, for the "owner" of the site could sell his water to others.

Streets developed too. The "street" from the south gate into the stockade was called Main. The street from the north gate was Market, so called because of the businesses that sprang up along this avenue. Property, or shebang sites, along Market Street were pricy. Some of the men who had staked a claim to a plot of ground there rented it out to others.

Wirz had prohibited the guards from bartering or selling items to the prisoners—and for good reason. A few Union greenbacks (dollars) could bribe a guard into supplying a prisoner with a knife or a gun or a shovel for digging. For the same reason, Wirz did not allow citizens of nearby Americus to enter the stockade without written permission. Even so, the "city" that was growing inside the stockade had its occasional tourist or visitor. Some residents of Americus and the surrounding countryside applied for permission to enter the stockade, finding that the trading opportunities were worth a few minutes of its nauseating stench.

Wirz did allow one other means of supplying outside goods to the prisoners. He authorized a local resident, James Selman, to be the camp sutler, or grocer. Selman's small store was a shack made of scrap lumber just inside the north gate at the head of Market Street. He dug a cellar in the ground to store vegetables such as onions and potatoes as well as to protect his inventory from theft during the night.

Prisoners who had money or who could barter some needed object for money could purchase additional food from the sutler. But the sutler's price was often quite high. Eggs, which might have sold in Macon or Atlanta for two dollars a dozen, cost five dollars—for just one egg—inside Andersonville. A pint (0.5 liter) of black beans that could be made into a tasty and nourishing soup sold for

Artist James E. Taylor sketched this business transaction of a prisoner trading his buttons for fresh peppers. The seller is probably James Selman, a local resident who had official permission to enter the stockade and trade with the prisoners.

forty cents. Blackberries, which grew wild in the woods beyond the stockade, sold for sixty cents a pint. Selman purchased his supplies from the residents of nearby Americus, who brought their eggs and molasses, watermelons and onions, sometimes sugar and coffee to Anderson Station. Prisoners who could do so patronized the sutler. But many prisoners were angry that Wirz was not providing sufficient food, forcing them instead to use their precious valuables for everyday necessities.

⋆⟶⊂⊃⟵⋆

Staying alive also meant keeping the mind healthy. Prisoners noted in their diaries that men who had lost hope seemed to die within weeks, even days. But many prisoners avoided depression by creating diversions to fill the many hours that remained in each day after roll call, after daily cleaning and delousing of clothing, after scavenging firewood and making mush, and after caring for the sick. Those who had pen and paper wrote in their diaries, commenting mostly on the food and the weather, and the sick and the dying. Some wrote letters home. Wirz had hung a wooden postbox inside the stockade. His prison staff read all letters and eliminated any details they considered to be too critical of the Confederacy. Letters sent north on a train might not reach their final destination for many weeks or months. Some letters were never delivered.

Men fashioned playing cards from paper. Others gambled with dice—or with the uncooked peas they sometimes got for rations. John McElroy carved chess pieces from pine roots. Others read, if they had brought a book into the pen with them or could barter for one. They read and then reread again and again until the soiled pages were soggy and stained. A number of men inside the stockade had Bibles. One prisoner had secured a copy of *Grey's Anatomy*, a medical encyclopedia. He read it twice.

Perhaps the prisoners' main preoccupation was plotting their escape. Some men devised clever plans for getting through the stockade gates without being shot. One disguised himself as a Confederate guard, having bartered some clothing. He got no farther than Wirz's headquarters when one of the guards spotted him for who he was—a Yankee bluecoat. Another lay down with the dead at the south gate and was carried outside in the charnel wagon. Many ran away while working outside the stockade to gather wood. The hounds usually found them. They returned exhausted and sometimes badly bitten by the dogs. Their punishment was being bucked and gagged or put in chains.

The greater number of prisoners, however, planned to escape through tunnels. Digging not only occupied men's time but also challenged their ingenuity. Shovels were hard to find, though a few prisoners had them. Most tunnelers relied on found objects for excavation—an oyster shell, a pocket knife, or a strip of scrap iron from a

Confederate authorities at Andersonville relied on dogs to track escaped prisoners. The horror of being caught is depicted in this engraving reprinted from *Life and Death in Rebel Prisons* published by prisoner Robert H. Kellogg in 1867.

bucket. The men formed secret pacts and took turns digging, first downward and then horizontally in the direction of the stockade fence and the pine forest beyond. Only one body at a time could fit inside these wormholes. Removing the soil was another challenge. Men carried out the dirt in a handkerchief or the sleeve of a shirt. They carried it concealed through the camp to deposit it in the bog near the creek or to put it down one of the camp's wells.

During the day, the men camouflaged their tunnels so that guards and "tunnel rats" would not spoil their escape plan. Tunnel rats were informers—prisoners who told the guards about the location of a tunnel. In exchange for this information, the rats received an extra ration or some other favor, perhaps chunks of wood for cooking. One prisoner, Samuel Burdick of Iowa, recalled how four prisoners dug a water well 60 feet (18 m) deep. About 20 feet (6 m) down, they began to tunnel horizontally for the stockade wall. Days before their intended escape, another prisoner betrayed them for a single plug of tobacco.

At night, while hundreds of prisoners were tunneling to freedom, hundreds of others gathered to pray and sing hymns. The men's voices rose and drifted across the stockade. The singing comforted many lying in their shebangs, including Ransom, who thought the stockade had a fair share of fine voices.

> *My heavenly home is bright and fair,*
> *Nor pain nor death can enter there;*
> *Its glittering towers the sun outshine,*
> *That heavenly mansion shall be mine.*
> *I'm going home, I'm going home,*
> *I'm going home to die no more;*
> *To die no more, to die no more,*
> *I'm going home to die no more.*

⊹⟫⟬⟬⟰

Those men who believed they had no control over their lives, no way to improve their wretched condition, slipped into depression. The surgeons at Andersonville called it "nostalgia," or homesickness.

Nostalgia was not just a longing for home. It was a dark, hopeless feeling of never being able to go home again. It lowered the body's vitality, the doctors believed. They noted that men in this state of mind seemed more likely to become ill. Wirz, too, commented on the growing despondency of the prisoners in the summer of 1863. In a letter to a superior officer, informing him of conditions within the stockade, he wrote, "A long confinement has depressed the spirits of thousands, and they are utterly indifferent."

The men's indifference showed itself in various ways. The despondent stopped eating, tossing away the bland, coarse cornmeal of their daily diet. Others could not chew the unsifted cornmeal because scurvy had infected their gums. Men stopped cleaning themselves and their clothing. Many no longer bothered to make the long trek to the sinks at the bottom of the hillsides. Instead, they fouled the ground where they cooked and slept. The camp grew filthier. The stench was sickening, literally. The men could not escape it—it permeated their air, their bodies, and their food.

Others lost interest in the welfare of their friends. One prisoner observed that the personalities of his comrades had changed. "They were not so ready to help each other," he wrote, "And do that which would in the least lessen one's own chances or advantages." Selfishness wasn't the cause. Before imprisonment, the men had not been selfish. Rather, the prisoner wrote that he believed human beings had an instinct for self-preservation. To survive, they shut out others and looked out only for themselves.

"CRAWLING TO FREEDOM"

For ten days, John Ransom had not written in his diary. On April 15, 1864, he wrote about visiting sick prisoners and feeling overwhelmed with despair. His next entry was April 26, 1864. What had happened to Ransom during that time? For the first five days, he and a few other men dug a tunnel. On the sixth day—or rather night—Ransom and three of the men crawled to freedom. Under the cloak of night, they ran for the pine forest. But they were weak with hunger and out of shape. Ransom could not run very far.

By dawn, he heard the baying of the hounds. When the dogs reached them, they circled and sniffed, but they did not bite. The guards appeared soon after, and Ransom's few hours of freedom ended. Wirz sentenced the escapees to two days in chains. At least they were chained in shade, and the guards gave him food.

In his July report to the War Department, Wirz reported that he had discovered eighty-three tunnels, some as deep as 20 feet (6 m) under the ground and varying from 10 to 140 feet (3 to 43 m) long. For all that digging, however, most who escaped through the tunnels were soon apprehended. Still, digging continued relentlessly—day after day.

Most men who crawled to freedom through the secret tunnels were recaptured within days. On a sweltering August night in 1864, a prisoner named Charles Hopkins crawled "like a snake" through the tunnel he had helped to dig. Once outside, he crawled through briars and pine needles and swampland. Hopkins fled with four others. Their hope was that the mud of the swamps would make their scent difficult to track. But the hounds found them anyway. Hopkins had strength enough to climb a tree, but one of the men with him did not. According to Hopkins's account, the dogs attacked him, tearing into his flesh. Within minutes, the guards appeared and called off the dogs. They ordered Hopkins at gunpoint out of the tree. He, too, made the sorrowful walk back through the swamp and the forest to the stockade. Hopkins not only survived his dog bites but also his imprisonment in Andersonville.

At night there was less singing among the men. Rumors of exchange no longer sparked any hope. Nostalgia "broke them down." Men wandered about the stockade with vacant eyes. Hundreds more lay motionless in their burrows or under their tattered shebangs and simply waited for death. "Hope and courage were the best physicians," observed one prisoner. When new prisoners arrived, standing dumbfounded inside the gate, he would tell them that a healthy mind was a hopeful mind. "Be hopeful, be courageous," he advised.

But often the new arrivals succumbed to nostalgia more quickly than the inmates who had been inside the stockade for months. They whimpered and cried. They called for their mothers. Some lost a sense of reality, talking to family members who weren't there or giggling at nothing at all. Others wondered not if but when death would come to them. Often, men who had been healthy when they arrived at Andersonville died.

This A. J. Riddle photo was taken in August 1864, a month when more that three thousand prisoners died. The men gathered at the center are receiving their rations from a wagon.

In mid-June, a few weeks after he had arrived in Andersonville, Warren Goss reported seeing a one-legged man drop his crutch near the deadline. The man put his hand on the rail to reach down for the crutch. When he did, a sentry shot him dead. Goss's version of the death of the prisoner known as Chickamauga differs from what other prisoners say they saw. One said Wirz ordered the sentry to shoot the man. Another swore Wirz took aim with his revolver and shot the prisoner himself. One said it happened in May. Another said June.

Robert Kellogg didn't actually see what happened. He heard a gunshot. He later saw Chickamauga lying inside the deadline. The story Kellogg heard was that Chickamauga was a tunnel rat and that he had fled beyond the deadline to escape being hanged by his own men.

James Page saw and heard what happened. A mob of perhaps one hundred or more prisoners had chased Chickamauga to the deadline. They suspected him of "blowing" on them, that is, telling Wirz the location of a tunnel on which they had worked for weeks. The one-legged man scrambled under the railing into the dead zone. He hobbled back and forth on his crutch, demanding to be taken to Wirz.

The mob taunted the sentry on the platform. He was new, a young boy with the Georgia Home Guard. He ordered Chickamauga back. He did not want to shoot him, he said. "Tin soldier," the mob mocked the boy guard.

The commotion inside the stockade had caught the attention of other guards, and soon Wirz arrived. He stepped through the south gate. Angrily, he demanded to know why Chickamauga was in the dead zone. The prisoners were going to kill him, the crippled prisoner answered. He'd rather be shot by a rebel guard than killed by his own men. Page said Wirz assured the prisoners that Chickamauga was innocent. Then Wirz left.

But Wirz remembered the incident differently. He later said that he removed his revolver from its holster and threatened to do what Chickamauga had asked—shoot him. This frightened the man, and a few of his fellow prisoners dragged him back over the line into camp. Wirz turned to the sentry and ordered him to shoot anyone who crossed the deadline.

After Wirz left, Chickamauga once again scrabbled into the dead zone. He sat down. Again, the boy guard ordered him back. The prisoner did not move.

"Tin soldier," the prisoners mocked the guard. "Wooden soldier!"

And then the crack of a gunshot echoed across the stockade.

John McElroy said the bullet took away Chickamauga's jaw. Goss said the bullet pierced his lung. Both men agreed on one point: the bullet did not at once kill Chickamauga. Goss remembered watching him writhe on the ground. No one dared to cross the deadline to help him.

On the platform, the sentry put down his smoking gun and covered his face with his hands. Wirz also heard the shot. He hurriedly climbed the ladder to the sentry post and looked down. Chickamauga lay bleeding on the ground.

The prisoner known as Chickamauga was a Canadian immigrant named Thomas Herburt, who had enlisted in the Union army. He had earned his nickname during the Battle of Chickamauga, Georgia, in September 1863. His wounds from that battle resulted in the amputation of his right leg below the knee. Herburt's death became a frequently told story about the horrors of Andersonville. As rumors spread from one shebang to another that day, the truth of what happened became unclear. Most prisoners found it easy to believe that Wirz, who had a foul mouth and quick temper, had murdered just another damned Yankee. Many swore they saw him standing on the sentry platform from which the fatal shot had come.

The Confederate victory in the Battle of Chickamauga, fought September 19–20, 1863, was a significant setback for the Union army. Andersonville prisoner Thomas Herburt was wounded in the fight.

Perhaps it was easier for the prisoners to blame Wirz than it was to admit that bluecoats were turning against bluecoats inside the pen. Chickamauga was an unpopular man in camp, in part because he talked endlessly, even when no one would listen to him. He seemed to be a favorite of the guards or perhaps of Wirz, for he often had permission to leave the stockade for hours. He had been a prisoner for eight months and had no talents to sell within the stockade. All he had to trade was information. It was his way of staying alive. But others saw it only as a betrayal.

Herburt died hours after suffering his wound. The incident seemed to disgust Page. He would later write, "The clamor and violence of our prisoners . . . drove a poor, heartbroken, one-legged fellow-prisoner to his death."

HOSPITAL GANGRENE AND SURGICAL FEVERS

Amputation was a common and dangerous surgery performed during the U.S. Civil War. Historians estimate that surgeons performed as many as fifty thousand amputations—on the battlefield, in hospitals, and in prisoner-of-war camps. Many amputees survived their surgeries. Many did not. Often the patient died not from the amputation itself but from complications that developed afterward, especially from what was known as hospital gangrene.

William Hale was not a physician. He was an Andersonville prisoner from New York State who worked in the stockade's hospital. Hale described his position as "master of the gangrene ward." Gangrene is the rotting away of flesh. In a place such as Andersonville, Hale stated, where starvation and scurvy had sapped men's strength, the appearance of gangrene "was the sure precursor of speedy death." Hale noted that within thirty-six hours after undergoing an amputation, the patient whose wound developed a putrid-smelling black spot was a "sure candidate for the trench."

Surgical fevers, on the other hand, took a few days longer to develop. After surgery, a wound might ooze odorless pus. Civil War surgeons believed this was a sign that the tissue was repairing itself. If the wound suddenly stopped oozing, dried up, and was followed by a high fever, mortality was almost certain. What doctors did not know then was their use of unsterile instruments during the surgery caused infection.

In fact, Civil War doctors knew nothing about bacteriology and the spread of germs. They did not wash their hands before operating on a patient. Nor did they sterilize their scalpels and saws. They wiped their

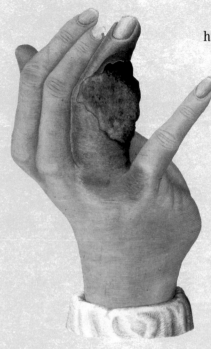

hands and their tools on bloody and pus-stained aprons. They washed a wound with a sponge that they had used on multiple patients, rinsing and then squeezing it in a basin of bloody water.

Doctors of the era did not understand the biological process that causes gangrene. In modern times, physicians classify gangrene into two categories: dry and wet. Dry gangrene is the result of a reduction in blood flow to a part of the body. Without nourishing blood, the tissue becomes cold and black and dry. Eventually, the tissue dies. Wet or moist gangrene is the result of an untreated infected wound. The body's infection-fighting white cells travel through the bloodstream to the site of the wound and begin to work. If the infection worsens or remains untreated, the tissue around the wound swells. The swelling, in turn, slows or stops the flow of blood (and the white blood cells) to the wound. The infection spreads and the tissue dies.

Gangrene is a medical term used to describe the death of tissue in an area of the body. The dead tissue often turns black or green and emits a bad odor.

Even if doctors at Andersonville had understood the causes of gangrene and surgical fevers, the lack of medical supplies and clean water would have hampered their efforts to perform sterile operations. And even if sanitary conditions could have been attained, the poor health of the patient prior to surgery increased the risk that he would die.

CHAPTER FIVE

THE RAIDERS AND THE REGULATORS

Wuld that I was an artist & had the material to paint this camp & all its horrors or the tongue of some eloquent Statesman and had the privleage of expressing my mind to our hon[orable] rulers at Washington, I should gloery to describe this hell on Earth where it takes 7 of its occupiants to make a shadow.

—SERGEANT DAVID KENNEDY,
ANDERSONVILLE PRISONER, JULY 9, 1864

In June 1864, the rain began. At first, the downpours were a relief. Rain washed the filth away. Day after day, the skies clouded over, and rain continued to fall. Men covered themselves with blankets and coats, but these materials were soon saturated and offered little protection from the blowing wind. The hillsides were thick with mud. Men who had dug burrows for protection from the sun crawled into holes that filled with water. Some burrows collapsed under the soaking rains. Unless a man crawled out quickly with the help of a friend, he could suffocate. Men without any shelter at all simply lay down in the mud to sleep.

"Raining yet," wrote Charles Hopkins in his diary on June 13, 1864, "and a most cold and dreary one too. Making the night too miserable for any brute to sleep." Five days later, he noted again in his diary, "Raining is the days duty . . . the rain was told to clear up, but no use."

For twenty-one days, it rained. The creek swelled and flooded the latrines. Human waste floated several inches deep beyond the creek.

Rain was a frequent occurrence at Andersonville. In her report to the government after her 1865 visit to Andersonville, Clara Barton described the effect of rain washing down the hillsides as so foul and loathsome as to fall short of reality.

Amid this deluge, on the seventeenth day of June, General John L. Winder arrived to take command of Andersonville. His transfer from Virginia to Georgia was not so much a promotion as a way to rid the Confederate capital of his dictatorial control. Local residents read in the *Richmond Dispatch* of the general's departure: "Thank God that Richmond is at last rid of old Winder; God have mercy on those to whom he has been sent."

The condition of the camp alarmed even the hardened general. The rain had created mudslides and had caused human sewage to contaminate the stockade. But the general was more disturbed by the lack of military discipline. In April when Winder had visited the camp, Lieutenant Colonel Persons had commanded the guards. They were Georgia soldiers, trained and drilled. When the War Department ordered the 55th Georgia into battle, however, the replacement guards at Andersonville came from the local militia (citizen army).

A native of Maryland, John Henry Winder was a graduate of West Point. He resigned his U.S. commission in 1861 to join the Confederate army. He was made a brigadier general and put in charge of Belle Isle and then Andersonville.

This home guard consisted of men too old or weak for the infantry (army of foot soldiers) and young farm boys who could neither read nor write and had no battlefield experience. More often than not, the target caught in the crosshairs of their old and often rusty rifles had been opossums and squirrels. The home guard did not have uniforms. Sometimes, they allowed prisoners to escape. Sometimes, they would shoot a man simply for reaching under the deadline for water. Wirz regarded the new guards as worse than worthless. He described them with disgust as "perfectly undrilled and undisciplined."

On the day after his arrival, General Winder began writing official letters. He requested additional military troops to guard the stockade. He strongly urged the construction of a second camp to end the overcrowding at Andersonville. Meanwhile, something had to be done about the filth and lawlessness inside the stockade.

✦⟐⟐✦

Each night from the sentry boxes atop the stockade, the guards called the hour. "Post number one. Ten o'clock and all's well!" From the next box, the guard answered, "Post number two. Ten o'clock and all's well." Around the stockade, the voices hollered, one after the other. Sometimes a guard changed the refrain: "General Lee's fallin' back and all's well" or "Here's your mule and all's well."

Inside the stockade, however, all was *not* well. Other sounds haunted the camp at night: groans of the sick and wounded, whimpers of the homesick, and the baying of the hounds tracking the scent of an escaped bluecoat. Prisoners heard sounds even more frightening than those of the dogs: the startled cries of men being ambushed in the dark or attacked inside their shebangs. On Belle Isle, Willie Collins and his thugs had preyed on the weak. At Andersonville his gang, known as the Raiders, had grown and numbered in the hundreds. The Raiders attacked their fellow prisoners to steal their goods. With stolen blankets, they kept warm. With stolen watches, they bartered with the guards. With stolen money, they bought vegetables and berries. Organized into bands, each led by a chieftain, the Raiders became bolder and more violent. In May and June, they began to attack during the day as well as at night. If a victim resisted, the thugs pummeled him with a club or brass knuckles, weapons the Raiders had somehow managed to smuggle into the stockade. While other men inside the pen weakened from malnutrition, the Raiders remained relatively healthy.

The Raiders shadowed their victims in the daytime. They noted the arrival of "fresh fish," befriended the new arrivals, and offered assistance in finding a good place to sleep. They lured their victims to their tent with the offer of selling a blanket or bucket. Once inside, the raiders knocked the victim to the ground, held a knife or razor to his throat, and demanded whatever money or valuables he might have. Some in the gang were spotters. They wandered through the crowded pen during the day, noting who had possessions and where they might have stashed them. They reported this information to the chieftains. Then, at night, the thugs attacked. A voice cried out, "Raiders!" If a man's comrades were nearby, the attack might be thwarted. "Get him!" voices shouted. If the rebel guards at their posts heard these cries of alarm, they did nothing to protect the prisoners. The prisoners would have to protect themselves.

One morning in June 1864, James Page walked toward the sinks. Although he never drank the foul-smelling water in the creek, his habit was to wash as best he could. As he made his way around the shebangs and down the hillside, he came upon the body of a man whose throat had been slit. The gaping wound at the man's throat suggested the murder weapon had been a razor. Although he had no proof at all, Page was certain the Raiders had murdered the man during the night.

The stockade society—with its neighborhoods, businesses, and even prayer meetings—lacked a police force. A reign of terror was how some men described life inside the stockade during May and June. Something had to be done. Most everyone knew who the Raiders were. And most knew, too, that their gangs were swelling in numbers. But who would dare point them out and risk having his throat slit with a razor in the dark? Among the thousands of fresh fish who entered the stockade in June was a young man who would take that risk.

> A REIGN OF TERROR WAS HOW SOME MEN DESCRIBED LIFE INSIDE THE STOCKADE DURING MAY AND JUNE.

On June 16, John W. Urban entered the gates of Andersonville. He gaped in horror at what he called a "hell-hole." The rain was relentless, and the mud was ankle deep. So crowded was the space that Urban could not believe there was room for even one more man. The gates closed behind him just the same.

Urban plowed through the mud, searching for a place to lie down. Whenever he spied empty ground, the men nearby told him it was taken already and to move on. At last he came to a plot near a squad of men from West Virginia who had been inside the stockade since March. They had a long pine log and offered Urban a place to rest. Sitting upon a log would at least keep him from lying in the mud. Although grateful, Urban thought he would never be able to survive such a horrible place. In the days that followed, the sun broke through. As his clothes began to dry, Urban's spirits lifted. He mustered the courage to make the best of things. And like so many others inside Andersonville, he consoled himself with this thought: "Our government would find out the terrible condition of our prison and . . . [take] measures . . . to release us."

Urban soon learned the meaning of the deadline. He heard, too, the rumors about the Raiders. This gang of lawless roughs, he heard, robbed newcomers to benefit themselves. Urban found it hard to believe that Union soldiers would brutalize one of their own. He believed that men who fought side by side on the battlefield would surely maintain their bounds of loyalty inside the prison pen. Surely, the stories the men told him were exaggerations. He soon learned otherwise.

⋆⇒◯⇐⋆

"Who wants to buy a watch?" John Scarsfield shouted as he moved among the shebangs on the hillside.

A prisoner known as John Dowd stepped out from under his shelter. He was holding his pants in his hands. He had been delousing them, pinching and singeing the lice from the seams. "How much?"

"Twenty dollars."

Dowd looked at Scarsfield's timepiece and rejected it. He already had a watch, on a silver chain. Scarsfield wandered away. He'd gotten what he wanted: information. Dowd, a fresh fish, not only had money to spend but also a watch.

Scarsfield returned a short time later and tried once again to interest Dowd in buying the watch. With Scarsfield this time was a short, burly fellow, known as Murphy. He had long side whiskers and a mustache. All at once, he tore the pants from Dowd's hands. With a knife, he slit the pocket and retrieved the watch on its silver chain.

Dowd spun around and grabbed Murphy by the throat. Suddenly, Dowd suffered a crushing blow. Scarsfield had stuck him with brass knuckles. Dowd fell. Scarsfield was on him, holding a dagger to his throat. "If you resist, I'll cut out your heart and throw it in your face!" Dowd did resist, and other Raiders quickly surrounded him. They kicked him repeatedly in the stomach, in the ribs, and in the head, leaving him bleeding on the ground.

Years later, John Urban would write his own account of that day's assault. It varied somewhat in the details. In his account, he was the man known as "Dowd." Why he had given Dowd as his name is unclear. Perhaps, like many men, he did so to gain two rations instead of one—reporting for roll call as John W. Urban and then also as Dowd. The watch on the silver chain belonged to a friend, and he was only holding it for him. That would explain why he might have been interested in Scarsfield's watch. He had gone to the creek for water, he said, when Scarsfield and the Raiders jumped him. Urban had fought back, hard, but still, the Raiders overpowered him. Urban's cries of "Murder!" brought men to his aid, some of whom wielded clubs. They saved his life. Urban did not know then who they were. Within days, however, the entire prison population would refer to them as the Regulators.

The incident might have ended there, but Urban was a hardened soldier. He had not survived two years on battlefields across Virginia and Maryland to succumb to a group of thugs among his fellow soldiers. Bleeding from a knife wound in the head and badly bruised about his face, arms, and legs, he appealed to the rebel guards. They summoned Wirz to the gate. He saw Urban's physical condition and listened to his account of the crime. Wirz swore, "By God, until every scoundrel of that gang is brought out of the stockade, I swear I shall not permit a single ration to be sent into the stockade."

Other prisoners agreed in their accounts of the event that Wirz was furious. He threatened to withhold rations from the entire population of the camp for a week unless the guilty Raiders were apprehended. But withholding rations wasn't necessary. Inside the stockade, because Urban had the courage to speak up, justice was about to be served.

◦━◦⊂━◦

The prisoners at Andersonville described the leader of the Regulators as an imposing figure: tall, broad shouldered, and tough. He was one of the old inmates, having arrived in early March when the stream was still clean. He lived in a hole that he had burrowed into the north hillside. His blanket shaded the entrance to his cave. James Page knew him as James Laughlin, or Limber Jim. Civil War historians believe the man was Sergeant Leroy Key from Bloomington, Illinois.

John McElroy knew Key quite well, as they were from the same battalion. He thought him one of the bravest men he had ever known. Weeks earlier, Key had begun to form his own secret police force at Andersonville. He recruited men to join him, swearing them to secrecy. McElroy was not nearly as large or strong as some of the others—Key was 6 feet 2 (1.9 m). But McElroy was willing to do his part. So, too, apparently was Wirz. After Urban's beating, Key somehow communicated

The honest prisoners did the best they could to fight off the bullies and criminals in their midst. But the Raiders were well organized and well armed and had the upper hand until the Confederate captors and the Regulators intervened.

with Wirz—perhaps through one of the rebel guards. He asked permission for the Regulators to bring to justice those responsible for the lawlessness inside the stockade. He promised to deliver the raiders to Wirz. After some consideration, Wirz not only agreed to the plan but also ordered the distribution of clubs to Key's men.

In all, Key's Regulators numbered more than one hundred men. One night, soon after Urban's beating, Key sent a message to his captains to move in force to arrest the Raiders in the morning. McElroy could hardly sleep. From the Raiders' shebangs on the south hillside, he heard singing and laughter. If they had gotten wind of Key's plan, they certainly were not losing any sleep over it.

On the appointed July morning, the blue sky was clear and sunny. The Regulators gathered and started down the north hillside. McElroy looked over his shoulder, surprised by the thousands of faces— men just standing, waiting. For once, the pen was silent.

The Regulators crossed the creek to the south bank. The Raiders were waiting there. They had formed a solid line across the pen with their leaders dead center. The two lines stepped closer. And then the Raiders surged forward. The fighting began. Men tangled, and the enraged Regulators clubbed the Raiders to their knees. As each captured Raider was dragged to the rebel guards at the gates, a cheer went up from the hillside spectators.

Many of the Raiders fled and hid in holes in the ground. Once discovered, they were dragged out and pummeled. The Regulators confiscated money, blankets, uniforms, watches, dishes, and food from within their shebangs.

"The raiders fight for their very life, and only taken after being thoroughly whipped," Ransom wrote. "A number killed." The Confederate guards at their posts were nervous, but they held their fire and let the Regulators do their "good work," as Ransom put it. That afternoon Wirz did not risk opening the gates for the ration wagon, though it had been loaded and was ready. The explosive atmosphere inside the stockade could backfire on him, and the empowered Regulators could overwhelm the guards. He sent the wagon away.

<hr/>

Ransom wrote in his diary: "Night. Thirty or forty of the worst characters in camp have been taken outside, and still the good work goes on. No food to-day and don't want any."

By the next morning, more than one hundred Raiders had been arrested. Among them was Willie Collins, a man who called himself Mosby, after a Confederate officer who was known for harassing Union troops on the battlefield. Arrested, too, were John Scarsfield and Seaman Andrew Muir, a recent arrival who had been lured into the Raiders in exchange for the promise of a dry place to sit and a little food to eat. Wirz called for the Union sergeant of every prisoner squad of ninety to report to his headquarters. He read to them General Orders No. 57, signed by General Winder, which granted the prisoners' earlier request for a trial to bring whomever to justice. The sergeants cheered. From among the sergeants, Wirz selected a jury. A sergeant was named judge, and still others took on the roles of prosecuting and defense attorneys.

Meanwhile, a less official form of punishment was being enacted inside the stockade. Arrested Raiders who had not committed serious offenses were being sent, one at a time, back into the stockade to face a gauntlet (a form of physical punishment). To form the gauntlet, the haggard but angry prisoners stood shoulder to shoulder in two long lines facing one another. They held whatever weapons they could find—pine boughs and sticks—to beat the Raiders. The rebel guard released the Raiders one at a time into the line of men. The Raiders had

Willie Collins adopted the name of Cavalry battalion commander John Singleton Mosby. Also known as the Gray Ghost, the real Mosby was known for his quick raids and his ability to elude his Union army pursuers.

GENERAL ORDERS NO. 57

Wirz took seriously the matter of John Urban's brutal beating and the necessity to rid the stockade of the Raiders. Wirz had reported the incident and the worsening situation to his superior officer, General John H. Winder. Winder issued the following order:

> Camp Sumter, Andersonville, GA., June 30, 1864
>
> "General Orders No. 57.
>
> "A gang of evil-disposed persons among the prisoners of war at this post having banded themselves together for the purpose of assaulting, murdering, and robbing their fellow-prisoners, and having already committed all of these deeds, it becomes necessary to adopt measures to protect the lives and property of the prisoners against the acts of these men, and in order that this maybe accomplished, the well-disposed prisoners may, and they are hereby authorized to, establish a court among themselves for the trial and punishment of such offenders. . . .
>
> "The proceedings, finders, and sentence in each case will be sent to the commanding officer for record, and if found in order and proper, the sentence will be ordered for execution.
>
> "By order of Brig. Gen. John H. Winder."

In issuing this order, the general authorized the prisoners to take action without fear of punishment either from him or Wirz.

no choice but to run through the gauntlet. They could not break the line, so tight was it with angry men, eager to punish those who had terrorized them and stolen from them. Some returning Raiders were badly beaten. Prisoners swarmed over any Raider who was unfortunate enough to lose his footing. Some Raiders did not survive their injuries.

The trial of Raiders accused of more serious crimes began almost at once and continued for three days. John Urban was among the first witnesses. The members of the jury who had not seen the Raider attack him seemed surprised at the Raider's brutality. Urban's face and head were still swollen and badly bruised from his injuries. His legs and arms were cut, and he had suffered broken ribs. Urban identified John Scarsfield as the person who had stuck him repeatedly with brass knuckles. At the end of the first day of the trials, the jury found Scarsfield guilty and sentenced him to hang.

The trial continued for two additional days as witnesses came forward to give testimony about other Raider attacks. When Andrew Muir was called to the makeshift courtroom, his appearance was altered. He had tried to disguise himself by shaving his side whiskers and mustache. Even so, a prisoner named Newton Baldwin testified that he saw Muir attack Dowd. Baldwin also testified that he had previously witnessed Muir attack another man, a sergeant.

When the trials ended, the jury found five additional men, including Muir, guilty and sentenced them to hang as well: Patrick Delaney, John Sullivan, Charles Curtis, and Willie Collins. Curtis appealed the court's decision. General Winder agreed to meet with him and hear his appeal. Curtis was a deserter from the U.S. service, he told the general. Therefore, Union prisoners had no right to put him on trial. "I wish to be tried by Confederate officers," he said.

General Winder considered the evidence. "Very well," he said at last. "I cannot get Confederate officers to try you, but I shall try you myself, and from all that I have heard of your case, I shall order you to be shot. The Yankees have sentenced you to be hanged. Which do you choose?"

The Raiders had been tried, found guilty, and sentenced, all in agreement with General Orders No. 57, which Winder had signed. Wirz refused to carry out the sentence himself, however. He had promised a fair trial, and the men had received this. The execution of the sentence would be the responsibility of the prisoners. He turned the condemned men over to the Regulators inside the pen, providing them with enough wood to construct a gallows.

The prisoners heard that Wirz was returning the Raiders to the pen, and they cursed him. If let loose inside the stockade, they would surely seek vengeance against their accusers. But when the prison gates opened, the men saw the wagonload of wood. Throughout the morning of July 11, 1864—a sweltering hot day, according to Andersonville diarists—the men watched the Regulators hammer together a crude gallows. A few shaky steps nailed together led to a narrow platform, just a few planks wide. The crossbeam of the gallows was just high enough so that a man's feet would not touch the ground when the trapdoor below him was sprung. The rope was rotted, but there was enough for six nooses to hang from the crossbeam. While the construction continued, Wirz told the quartermaster that he would not issue rations that day. He feared the executions would excite the prisoners into rebellion.

Dozens of Andersonville accounts from surviving prisoners describe what happened late that same afternoon. The gates opened. Wirz rode his bay mare inside the stockade, ahead of the six condemned men. The captain addressed the population of the pen, all of whom it seemed had gathered as near the gallows as possible.

"Boys, I have taken these men out and now I return them to you, having taken good care of them. I now commit them to you. You can do with them as you see fit." He turned his horse so that he faced the

Frank Leslie's Illustrated Newspaper artist James E. Taylor captured the gruesome scene of the mass hanging of the Raiders.

condemned men. "May the Lord have mercy on your souls," he said. He pressed his heels into the belly of the mare and rode out through the gates.

James Page had found a place so near the gallows he could see Patrick Delaney smile as a Regulator slipped a noose around his neck, so near that he could hear Curtis ask Delaney how he intended to get out of this fix. "As for me, I'm going to make a break," he said.

Curtis had tucked a knife within his clothing, and then he pulled it and slashed right and left. He pushed through the crowd and fled. The Regulators pursued and eventually dragged him back to the scaffold. He was filthy, having sunk into the sewage along the creek. Someone gave him water, and he drank deeply.

Father Peter Whelan, a Catholic priest who frequently came inside the stockade to minister to the spiritual needs of the men, stood on the scaffold with them and pleaded with the prison population for their lives. No one else, it seems, spoke on the Raiders' behalf. Show mercy, the priest implored. But what mercy had the Raiders shown the weak and dying? None. And so the prisoners gave none to them in return.

"I do not think that any of them believed that they would have to die," John Urban would later write in his memoir. "When, however, they found it was to be a terrible reality, their firmness commenced to give way." The condemned looked upon the mass of prisoners before them with "helpless despair," wrote Urban.

Each man was allowed a few final words. Patrick Delaney said he'd rather die than live as they were forced to live inside the bull pen, like animals. Scarsfield said he had begun his evil ways by stealing food. His "evil associates" were to blame for his downfall. Curtis asked for forgiveness from his victims, but no one stepped forward to give it. Collins denied murdering anyone. He begged for his life. Andrew Muir was perhaps the most remorseful. He gave "a sad little speech about himself." He was just a "poor Irish chap," he said. He had never meant to harm anyone. He had never once thought that this would be his fate when he stepped through the gates of Andersonville. Only one, Sullivan, remained silent.

Key stepped forward. He stated that the time was up.

The executioners slipped a meal bag over each man's head. The accused stood on loose planks. At the moment of execution, two men pulled away the planks and the six Raiders fell. Five died right away. But the sixth, Collins, struggled. The frayed rope that held him snapped. Collins fell to the ground, still alive. A few voices cried out: "Don't hang him!" But the executioners led him up the rickety steps to the scaffold and hung him a second time.

For about thirty minutes, the bodies hung from the gallows. Men filed past to get a good look. Then the Raiders were taken down and carried outside the stockade.

Wirz witnessed it all from a sentry platform. "It is a sad sight to see six of our own men, who were fellow prisoners, suffer death in such an ignominious [disgraceful] manner," Urban stated, then added, "But their crimes were great."

Ransom wrote thoughtfully about what had happened and why. "It was an awful sight to see, still a necessity." He had known Mosby. He didn't believe he deliberately meant to kill anyone, but he had robbed sick prisoners of their blankets and rations. In Ransom's opinion, those cruel actions had resulted in the deaths of the victims.

Wirz appears to have granted the prisoners' request to bury the Raiders in a separate site. They did not want the men to be in the same cemetery as honorable Union soldiers who had died at Andersonville. Rumor later circulated that the men assigned to bury the Raiders had placed the bodies face down. It was the custom for executed criminals and the final retaliation.

Are the rules of war different on the battlefield than in the prison pen? Men like Leroy Key and John Urban would answer no. But Urban came to understand a grim truth about war and soldiering. "Most of the men who served in the Union army served from purely patriotic motives, and in the ranks could be found some of the best citizens in the country," Urban wrote. "But it is also true that quite a number went into the army more for the purpose of plunder than for any love they had for the country."

All classes of men passed through the gates of Andersonville in 1864. Some, like Sullivan, left behind their soldier's honor or perhaps never had it to begin with. But others were war's fatalities. Seaman Andrew Muir was in the wrong place at the wrong time. The prison pen, not the battlefield, destroyed him.

SCURVY

John Ransom was sick. His teeth were loose. His gums had swollen and were bloody. His legs were swollen, and he had little energy. Ransom knew what ailed him: scurvy. He had noticed the first signs of scurvy in May. By July he could not walk.

Throughout the Civil War, soldiers in the field as well as in prison camps in the North and the South suffered from scurvy. Lack of vitamin C in the diet causes scurvy, but Civil War doctors had no precise knowledge of vitamins and minerals. Still, they understood from experience that vegetables and fruits were foods that prevented and cured scurvy. The doctors called these foods antiscorbutics.

If the disease progresses untreated, many medical complications can develop. The body loses its ability to fight infection. The cords of the leg muscles tighten so that the legs become bent and the person is unable to walk. Internal bleeding is also a complication. So, too, is night blindness. Many men in Andersonville complained of "moon blindness." Scurvy was the cause.

"We all had scurvy, more or less," said John McElroy, "but as long as it kept out of our legs, we were hopeful." In early August, however, McElroy's symptoms were serious enough that he lined up with the others at the south gate in hopes of being admitted to the hospital. He had lost a great deal of weight, as had most of the men inside the stockade. He agreed with a fellow prisoner who said their legs looked like "darning needles stuck in pumpkin seeds." The physician looked McElroy over and then allowed him to pass out of the stockade to the hospital.

Wild blackberries were ripening on bushes in the woods, and Wirz had authorized prisoners to harvest as many as possible for the sick. Instead of going to the prisoners, the bulk of the berry harvest became wine, brewed and drunk by the nurses, who became intoxicated.

CHAPTER SIX

GENERAL EXCHANGE

It is hard on our men held in Southern prisons not to exchange them, but it is humanity to those left in the ranks to fight our battles. At this particular time to release all rebel prisoners would insure Sherman's defeat and would compromise our safety here.

—UNION GENERAL ULYSSES S. GRANT, AUGUST 18, 1864

In moments of despair, the Andersonville prisoners asked themselves why. Why had their government not agreed to an exchange? Why had the United States abandoned them in this place?

No one had an answer. Some men believed the War Department simply didn't know the truth about conditions within the camps. That was why they had not agreed to a prisoner exchange. But many others believed that the United States had chosen not to exchange prisoners. Some cursed President Abraham Lincoln and his secretary of war, Edwin Stanton, for abandoning them in the prison pens. Still others accused the Confederacy of postponing exchanges as a way to torment and intentionally kill prisoners or to persuade them to betray the Union and join the Confederate cause.

In fact, the prisoner exchange agreement between the North and the South had collapsed a year earlier in 1863. The North had cited reports of ill treatment of prisoners in Southern camps. The War Department refused to return healthy rebel prisoners for malnourished, diseased Yankees. Reports of suffering Union prisoners of war had made headlines in Northern newspapers.

There was another reason, however, why the North ended negotiations for exchange. It was a change in the Union's political and military policy on slavery. Slave labor was integral to the South's economy. "To save the Union the North had to destroy the Confederacy," explains Civil War historian Bruce Catton, "and to destroy the Confederacy it had to destroy slavery."

The change in policy had been made in January 1863, when President Lincoln signed a document called the Emancipation Proclamation. This single document gave freedom to all slaves held in rebellious states. (Lincoln and the Union refused to recognize the Confederacy as an independent nation.) It also stated that black men "will be received into the armed services of the United States." Soon after, recruitment posters for the U.S. Army began to

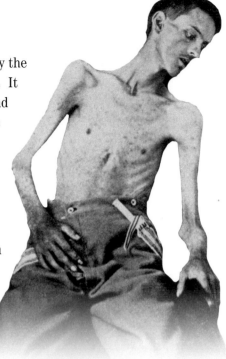

This photo of an emaciated prisoner recently released from a prison in the South shocked Northerners. Enraged citizens increased pressure on the Union government to deal with the prisoner-of-war problem immediately.

appear in public places in the North. "Rally, Men of Color, at Once for Your Country," the posters stated. Thousands of black men enlisted. By May 1863, African American soldiers were fighting on the battlefields in the South. They, too, became prisoners of war.

The Confederacy viewed the Emancipation Proclamation as an attempt to incite a slave uprising and therefore refused to release black prisoners of war. To do so meant recognizing that black men were equal to white men. To Southerners, who regarded enslaved blacks as property, this was unthinkable.

TWO BLACK SOLDIERS, ONE WHITE OFFICER

Black as well as white Union soldiers lived inside Andersonville. William Henry Jennings and John Fisher had enlisted in the 8th U.S. Colored Infantry Regiment, formed in Philadelphia, Pennsylvania. Both were captured after the Battle of Olustee in Florida in February 1864. Jennings suffered a wound in the thigh of his left leg, but he received no medical treatment—either from the Confederates who had captured him or from the surgeons inside the Andersonville stockyard. The Confederate officers forced the black soldiers into hard labor. They felled trees. They dug trenches and a well for water in the fort outside the stockade. White prisoners were not forced to do such work. Should the black soldiers refuse, their guards punished them severely.

"I was placed on duty about a month after I was put in the stockade," wrote Jennings. "I was set to digging a ditch outside the stockade. My wound was then bleeding. I was whipped in March 1864. I got thirty lashes by order of Captain Wirz. I was

A lithograph depicts black Union soldiers of the 8th U.S. Colored Infantry Regiment and their commanding officer, Colonel Charles W. Fribley (left).

whipped for not going to work one morning. I was unable to do so. I had caught a heavy cold, working in the water in the swamp. The lashes . . . were laid on by Turner, the man who ran the hounds. They whipped me on my bare back. They made me bend over. Afterward that took me and put me in the stocks. I was kept there a day and a night. I did not get any food or drink while in the stocks."

When John Fisher refused to work, the rebel guard gave him thirty-nine lashes. "The strap they whipped me with was two and a half feet [0.8 m] long and as broad as my three fingers," said Fisher. He knew of other African American soldiers who had also been punished this way. The men did not need to tell Fisher that they received lashings. He could see the evidence on their skin. "The whipping leaves upon the back the marks of the strap," he said.

Inside Andersonville, too, was white Union officer Major Archibald Boyle. Officers were not usually sent to Andersonville but rather to a separate camp in Macon, Georgia. But because Boyle had command of an African American regiment, the First North Carolina Volunteers, the Confederate officers refused to recognize his rank. When he entered the stockade in May 1864, he was still suffering from severe leg wounds. He made his way on crutches to the prison hospital, where a Union soldier, working as a hospital steward, began to bind his leg. Boyle was in full uniform, and so he was totally recognizable as the commander of the First North Carolina Volunteers. Upon seeing the treatment the officer was receiving, a doctor approached him. He ordered the steward to stop. "Send him out." he ordered.

Boyle looked hard at him, but he did not move. The hospital steward began again to bind the leg. The doctor turned away.

Boyle survived his imprisonment at Andersonville but his captors refused to recognize his rank as a Union officer. After the war in 1866, President Andrew Johnson promoted Boyle to the rank of lieutenant colonel, citing his gallant and meritorious serivces during the war.

The Confederacy threatened to raise the "black flag" in those battles in which African American soldiers fought. Raising the black flag was a signal on the battlefield that no prisoners of war would be taken. Soldiers who surrendered or were captured would instead be killed. In addition, the Confederate War Department threatened to execute, if captured, any white Union officer of a black regiment.

The South never actually hoisted the black flag. But with few exceptions, generally for officers of very high rank, the exchange of *all* prisoners ceased as a result of this bitter disagreement over black prisoners.

The men inside Andersonville were not just prisoners of war. They were prisoners of politics. As summer wore on and the situation grew even more desperate, the reasons why they were there weren't so important. All that mattered was getting out. If the Union government did not act soon, there would be no bluecoats left to exchange. They would all be dead.

The Union army made a strong effort to recruit African American soldiers as evidenced by this poster of the 1860s. Once in the army, however, they were paid less than their white counterparts and were often treated harshly.

<hr>

At a mass meeting inside the stockade in July 1864, the prisoners debated what to do. According to prisoner Prescott Tracy, some of the rebel sergeants who took roll call each morning suggested the prisoners draft a petition to send to Washington, D.C., explaining the hardships and requesting a speedy release. Soon after, a group of prisoners appealed to General Winder. Would he allow a committee to travel under a flag of truce to Washington, D.C., to deliver such a message personally to President Lincoln? The general agreed.

Some objected to the plan. An honorable soldier doesn't beg for his life, they believed. But the resolution drafted by the Union sergeants did not plead for mercy. It focused on the prisoners' patriotism and the government's obligation to honor those men who had rallied to defend the Union. In part, the resolution read:

> *No one can know the horrors of imprisonment in crowded and filthy quarters but him who has endured it, and it requires a brave heart not to succumb. But hunger, filth, nakedness, squalor, and disease are as nothing compared with the heartsickness which wears prisoners down, most of them young men whose terms of enlistment have expired, and many of them with nothing to attach them to the cause in which they suffer but principle and love of country and of friends. Does the misfortune of being taken prisoner make us less the object of interest and value to our Government? . . . These are no common men, and it is no common merit that they call upon you to aid in their release from captivity.*

Prescott Tracy was among the six men elected to travel north. The group boarded a train at Anderson Station on August 9. By then the population inside the stockade had topped thirty-three thousand. Andersonville had been a prisoner-of-war camp for just five months, and during that time, an estimated five thousand men had died.

THE TERRIBLE TRUTH?

Gruesome images of two Union prisoners of war appeared on the cover of the June 18, 1864, issue of *Harper's Weekly*. In both images, the men are partially clothed so that the reader can see the bones of their ribs and collarbones. In one image, a doctor has his hands around the soldier's neck. The man was so emaciated from his treatment in rebel prisons, the article explained, that he had no strength to lift or hold his head upright without help. The captions under those two photographs read: "Rebel Cruelty—Our starved soldiers."

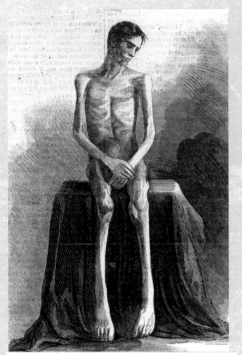

Union soldiers as they appeared on their release from rebel prisons were featured in *Harper's Weekly*, June 18, 1864.

The images were drawings made at a Union military hospital in Annapolis, Maryland. The soldiers had been released from Belle Isle. The article stated that the images were of "death in life" and "fearful to look at" but also evidence of a "terrible truth." That truth was that starvation and not disease had caused these men's bodies to waste away. The article explained that a congressional committee of the U.S. government had made a thorough investigation of the treatment of prisoners in rebel camps. The committee published eight photographs, each as gruesome as the two in *Harper's Weekly*. The photographs were evidence of a Confederate conspiracy to intentionally starve prisoners of war, the committee concluded.

Without question, the images of the soldiers were shocking. But were they representative of all prisoners in Southern camps? Stanton wanted the people of the North to believe it was. By inflaming their passions, Northerners would continue to support the war.

In September 1864, the U.S. Sanitary Commission published a lengthy report on the treatment of Union prisoners in rebel camps. The report was hundreds of pages long and included specific details that further horrified the public. Prisoners were robbed of their clothing and money as well as other valuables, even photographs of loved ones. Their rations were cornmeal with the cobs ground into it, worm-infested peas, and generally no more than 2 ounces (57 g) of meat.

While many of the details were true, the conclusion of a Confederate conspiracy was without proof. Still, the propaganda messages enabled Stanton to exact vengeance. In retaliation for the inhumane treatment of Union prisoners, he ordered reduced rations for the Confederate prisoners held in Northern camps. It was not the first time Stanton had reduced rations. But the further reduction mandated in January 1864 reduced the rations to a level where the men's health suffered significantly.

"We are now beginning to feel to some extent the vengeance of the Government of the United States. They have stopped our rations of sugar, coffee and candles. We get nothing but bread and meat with a few beans," wrote Confederate prisoner R. F. Webb in his diary. "This, of itself, is not so bad, had it not been for an outrageous order from Colonel Hill, holding each man responsible for any attempt to escape on the part of any prisoners by withholding entirely the rations, or in other words, starving us entirely unless we turn spies and informers upon our fellow prisoners."

Anthony Keiley, captured in Virginia and transported north to Elmira, wrote in his diary that the reduction in food was rapidly reducing the health of the inmates. Scurvy became, in Keiley's words, almost "an epidemic."

By August 14, the delegation had reached Union lines. Tracy gave a written statement to Union officers there, providing additional details about the stockade. Most of the men at Andersonville were nearly naked. Some men's clothing was simply meal bags with holes cut for the head and arms. "We have no shelter from sun, rain, or cold; no covering at night," he wrote. "Full one half are sick with malignant diarrhea and scurvy, the worst and most loathsome kind." The dead were found lying all over the camp, he continued. The surgeons could do little because they had no medicine.

> THE DEAD WERE FOUND LYING ALL OVER THE CAMP. THE SURGEONS COULD DO LITTLE BECAUSE THEY HAD NO MEDICINE.

Five days later, Tracy and the five other Andersonville prisoners were exchanged at Port Royal Ferry, South Carolina. The next stops on their journey north would be the military hospital at Annapolis, Maryland, and then, Tracy hoped, the White House.

If the War Department in Washington, D.C., knew little of the true horrors of Andersonville, the Confederate War Department in Richmond most certainly knew a lot. For months, Persons, Richard Winder, Wirz, and John Winder had documented the lack of rations and tools. They expressed the need for axes, buckets, nails, and shovels to improve the condition of the camp.

Richmond sent no additional doctors or medicines, no tents, and no blankets. Instead, they sent Lieutenant Colonel Daniel T. Chandler to inspect the camp. Chandler's report was as blistering as the

Georgia sun. The situation at Andersonville, both inside the stockade and outside in the hospital, required "prompt and decisive measures of relief. The discomforts and sufferings of the prisoners seem almost incredible," he wrote. The number of dead was shocking. While Chandler commended Wirz for his attempts to better the conditions, he condemned General Winder for his ineffectiveness and recommended that he be replaced.

In Richmond, Chandler's report passed through the hands of John B. Jones, a clerk in the War Department. He passed the document to the secretary of war, who, he presumed, would place it in the hands of President Davis. Whether that happened or not is unclear. But Jones would comment in his diary about the report, noting that its content was "ugly." Chandler had cited General Winder's treatment of the prisoners as "barbarous" and their condition as "hell on earth."

⋅⇒◐⇐⋅

At about the same time that the camp delegation was traveling to Washington, D.C., with a petition requesting the exchange of Andersonville's prisoners, the War Department in Richmond made a similar appeal. The Confederate agent for exchange of prisoners wrote to the agent of exchange in the United States. The Confederacy proposed releasing thousands of Union prisoners. In view of the great suffering these men were enduring, the Confederacy did not request an exchange of Confederate prisoners. The War Department asked only for the Union to provide transportation for the men under a flag of truce. Enclosed with the letter was a statement of the rate of mortality in Andersonville.

Weeks passed. The letter went unanswered.

The War Department in Richmond wrote two additional letters, emphasizing that they were not requesting a general exchange but rather transportation to return sick men to their homes. Finally, on

August 31, 1864, the assistant agent of exchange in the United States wrote back. "I have no communication on the subject from our authorities," his letter stated, "nor am I yet authorized to make any answer."

It wasn't a yes. But it wasn't a no, either. Still, with each day the War Department in Washington delayed its response to the request, more men died at Andersonville.

In August 1864, the outcome of the war was far from decided. Carnage continued on battle-fields. President Lincoln called for an additional half million volunteers for the military. "The men were needed," he said, "and must be had." Many in the nation, however, were crying for peace.

Prisoners from Andersonville arrived in Washington, D.C., in August 1864 to meet with President Abraham Lincoln *(above)*. This portrait of Lincoln was taken that year by famed Civil War photographer Mathew Brady.

On August 24, 1864, an editorial in the *New York Times* noted that four delegates from the Confederate prison camp known as Andersonville had arrived in Washington to meet with the president. "The statement that these men are prepared to lay before the president is horrifying," the editor wrote. "The duty of the military authorities is surely clear . . . see to the release of our brave and patriotic soldiers."[76] A few days later, the same newspaper printed on page 1 a lengthy statement from Union soldier Tracy, describing in grim detail the conditions inside the camp. Also included was a sketched map of the stockade, based on Tracy's observations. Missing from this article, however, was any word of the prisoners' meeting with President Lincoln.

Did the meeting occur? No record exists in official War Department documents stating that it did. That President Lincoln read the report sent from Andersonville and signed by the imprisoned sergeants is likely. In its mission to achieve an immediate general exchange, the delegation from Andersonville had failed. But in raising public awareness of the misery inside the stockade, the delegation had succeeded. Additional news articles and letters to the editor began to appear in Northern newspapers, demanding the government take action. The *New York Times* published a medical report sent by an assistant surgeon at Andersonville to his superior officer. Dying on the battlefield might be honorable, but families were increasingly unwilling to sacrifice their men held in prison pens. Pressure on the White House and the War Department increased that autumn of 1864. Community leaders as well as families wrote letters directly to President Lincoln: "We know you can have them exchanged if you give your attention to it," wrote one "political friend" of Lincoln. "It is simple murder to neglect it longer."

Families of the Andersonville prisoners could not imagine the depths of despair being experienced by their loved ones. But in 1864, hearing of the camp's horrendous conditions, many were spurred to write to the president pleading prisoner exchanges.

A LETTER TO LINCOLN: PRISONER EXCHANGE

Some men inside the Andersonville stockade feared that their government had abandoned them. Their families, however, had not. Many wrote letters to their congressmen, and some even wrote to President Lincoln, pleading for the Union to negotiate with the Confederate War Department to bring their men home.

Rushford, N.Y., September 12, 1864

Hon. A. Lincoln:

Sir: One of my boys, who is a prisoner of war in the hands of the enemy, and who was last heard from on Belle Isle, is now supposed to be in Andersonville, GA, if living, suffering for want of food and clothing; has a family here consisting of a wife and two children in indigent [poor] circumstances. Winter is approaching, and my said son and 30,000 more brave soldiers must perish unless the Government should relieve them by bringing about an exchange. I am an old man and can do nothing, but humanity prompts me to lay the case before you. . . . Mr. President, what can be done and what will you do to liberate them from this cruel bondage?

Respectfully, yours,

Samuel White

On occasion, Lincoln requested the exchange of an individual prisoner, usually a high-ranking officer. When it came to general exchanges of enlisted men, however, the president relied on the judgment of General Ulysses S. Grant, leader of the entire Union army. In a letter Lincoln wrote to Grant, dated October 5, 1864, he stated that Grant was "at liberty" to make the decision. Although Lincoln understood that being a prisoner of war was "cruel bondage," the president trusted that Grant's judgment would be for "the public good."

Photographer Mathew Brady took this photograph of Union general Ulysses S. Grant at Cold Harbor, Virginia, in 1864.

Grant's belief was that to reinstate prisoner exchange would prolong the war, because exchanged prisoners return to battle. The war then would become one of extermination. In Grant's mind, therefore, the greater public good was ending the war sooner. And that meant no exchanges.

CHAPTER SEVEN
LEAVING ANDERSONVILLE

"Hurrah! Hurrah! Hurrah!!! Can't holler except on paper. Good news. Seven detachments ordered to be ready to go at a moment's notice. . . . All who cannot walk must stay behind."

—JOHN RANSOM, SEPTEMBER 6, 1864

In the distance, John Ransom could see the tops of the pine trees. They swayed with the wind. The high stockade fence, however, prevented any cooling breeze from circulating inside the prison pen. With an advanced case of scurvy, John Ransom could no longer walk.

Built of tight-fitting pine logs, the stockade wall was so solid that even if the prisoners had been able to approach the outer wall, they would not have been able to see the outside world. The lighter inner fence known as the "deadline" was built approximately 19 to 25 feet (6 to 7 m) inside of the stockade.

Battese, his friend and former partner in the laundry business, carried him to the creek and helped him to bathe. But Ransom knew that if help did not come soon, he would go to the hospital and from there to a trench grave. His eyesight was very poor. Just to write in his diary took all his energy. He longed for a square of shade to lie in. Some days he fantasized about drinking a glass of iced lemonade. Instead, Battese dug roots to brew a tea for Ransom. He made a soup with bits of beef, onion, and potato. On those days when Ransom ate something nourishing, his spirits lifted. If he could avoid the hospital, he might yet survive.

A stockade fence, no matter how high, cannot prevent disease from spreading. A number of the ragtag guards outside the stockade suffered from some of the same infections as the prisoners. In early August, Wirz became ill to the point of collapse. "Wirz is very sick," General Winder noted in a report dated August 13, 1864. The general believed Wirz's illness was caused by overwork. "He ought to have gone to bed two weeks ago," the general wrote, "but kept up because he had none to whom the command could be turned over."

Exhaustion might have complicated Wirz's health, but his symptoms mirrored those of the prisoners who were dying from scurvy. Confederate soldiers who saw Wirz would later comment on how feeble and emaciated he appeared. As the days passed, he became weaker. He needed help to mount his horse and struggled to hold himself upright in the saddle. Finally, he stayed away from the camp entirely, unable to make the journey on horseback from his home. Lieutenant Samuel Boyer Davis came to Andersonville to take command, at least until Wirz recovered. The rumor had begun to spread through camp, however, that Wirz had died. In fact, Wirz was very near death. And more change was coming.

The storm came suddenly. About noon the August skies darkened from gray to black. Lightning flashed. Thunder cracked. Rain fell in torrents. So heavy was the downpour that the water wells the prisoners had dug filled and overflowed. The rapid runoff carved gullies in the hillsides. The creek through the stockade began to rise and overflow. The creek flowed out of the stockade at the east wall. But rain came so fast and hard that the water backed up, creating a putrid lake of human wastes. For two hours, the rain drenched the pen. Suddenly, under the force of the dammed-up water, the pine logs on the east wall of the stockade gave way. The water gushed forward, taking additional pine logs with it.

The storm had come so quickly and was so fierce that a breach in the stockade wall suddenly appeared—but the men were too weak and too surprised to flee. Witnesses would later state that the storm opened the stockade in at least six places. The guards rallied to the emergency, guns pointed on the prisoners below, preventing escape. But the prisoners seemed more interested in scavenging the logs for their own use than in trying to run away.

The rain continued that night, though not as hard. The guards began at once to rebuild the wall, closing the gaps. The men felt some satisfaction in knowing the rebels had to stand in that pouring rain, out from under their roofed sentry boxes. That night, at least, they got a taste of what it was like to be a prisoner without shelter in Andersonville.

The next day, much to the amazement of all inside the stockade, a spring bubbled from the ground midway up the north hillside. The water was pure and sweet, but it was also beyond the deadline. On one hand, that was a good thing, for it meant that no one individual owned it and so could not charge others for a taste. On the other hand, to venture beyond the railing was to risk being shot by a guard. The thirsty prisoners stood and stared. They began to devise ways to fish for drinks of the sweet, clean water by attaching cups to the ends of sticks.

This James E. Taylor sketch shows prisoners reaching across the deadline to capture freshwater from what came to be called Providence Springs. Eventually, they dug channels that routed the precious water into the camp area.

No doubt the storm had washed away enough soil to allow the natural springs to rise. One prisoner recalled a terrific bolt of lightning striking the ground, killing a number of prisoners. When he went to the spot, he saw a tear in the ground at the point the lightning had entered the earth. Many prisoners believed the sudden appearance of the lifesaving water was a miracle, God's answer to their prayers for release. As a result, the water source became known as Providence Springs, and negotiations soon resulted in digging a channel to direct the water into the camp.

Some prisoners would later recall that Wirz said the dirty creek water was good enough for Yankees. And perhaps he had. Nevertheless, negotiations soon resulted in digging a channel to direct the water beyond the deadline into the safe area of the camp. The police force that had been formed six weeks earlier protected the springs from contamination. In the diaries and memoirs of Andersonville survivors, Providence Springs was the highlight of August. More than one man believed his survival was due to Providence Springs.

⊷⊜⊶

One night in September 1864, as the guards shouted their rounds, John McElroy heard one holler, "Post Number Four, half past eight o'clock, and Atlanta's gone to Hell!"

McElroy couldn't believe his ears. The fall of Atlanta would be a Union triumph. Was the news a cruel trick? Had Union general William Tecumseh Sherman's troops at last pushed the Confederates out of Atlanta? The city was a major crossroads for the Confederacy, with four rail lines converging there. If Atlanta truly had "gone to Hell," then, the Confederacy was near its end.

McElroy was not the only man who heard the announcement, for within moments, a general cheer rose throughout the stockade. Unlike

Ransom, some prisoners had not yet lost their voices. That night small groups of men gathered. Some began to sing patriotic songs such as "The Star-Spangled Banner" and "Rally 'Round the Flag."

Most men had lost track of days and weeks. Was it after Atlanta fell—or just before—that the news of a general exchange spread like wildfire through the stockade? Perhaps this time, at last, the rumors of a general exchange were real. And yet, so many promises of exchange had been given and then broken that many men refused to believe it.

This time, however, proved different. This time, the gates of Andersonville swung open.

Not all could leave at once, of course. There simply wasn't transportation. They would depart Andersonville as they had arrived, in

In a final sketch for *Frank Leslie's Illustrated Newspaper*, James E. Taylor records the departure of the prisoners from Andersonville.

groups of hundreds, packed tightly in boxcars. Their destination was unknown. As men walked through the gates, their spirits soared. Surely the trains they boarded would take them out of the Georgia wilderness toward the sea where Union ships waited under flags of truce.

On September 6, Ransom wrote in his diary that seven detachments of prisoners had gone out the gate. His detachment was the tenth and would go the next day. There was a drawback, however. Those too ill to walk could not leave, the guards told them. Ransom could hardly stand upright on his own two feet. Walking out of the stockade was as impossible as being served a glass of lemonade. Still, Battese assured him that he would not leave him behind.

At midnight on September 7, 1864, Battese picked Ransom up and carried him to the gate. Ransom still had possession of the blanket out of which he had cheated a Confederate soldier so many months ago in Richmond. The prisoners fell into ranks of four. As they walked through the gates, the guards kept count. Battese placed Ransom in the middle between himself and another man to brace him upright. As they moved through the gate, Ransom said he heard a guard call after them. But Battese kept walking.

Robert Kellogg likewise shouldered a feeble comrade to help him pass through the gate. He recalled Wirz standing in front of his headquarters as they walked passed. "You'll never come back here again!" Wirz told them.

Although conditions in the prison camp at Millen, Georgia, were squalid, transferred prisoner James Madison Page must have found them a considerable improvement over those of Andersonville.

John McElroy left Andersonville soon after. He used his tent pole to walk. He took with him the overcoat that had served him hard for eight months and his crudely carved pine root chess pieces.

James Madison Page left Andersonville in mid-September, with Billy Bowles at his side. They were sent from Andersonville to a camp in Millen, Georgia. Page and Bowles were the only two survivors of the original eleven from Belle Isle. "It was a sad journey for Billy and I," Page wrote, "since we had to leave so many of our comrades . . . buried in the grave-yard; but we were going to be exchanged, so they said."

So they said.

"HELLMIRA" IN THE NORTH

On August 10, 1864, Union general William Hoffman issued Circular No. 4 to all commanders of prison camps in the North. Hoffman was the commissary general for all Union prison camps. This particular document prohibited sutlers from selling food to inmates. Packages of food sent by family members in the South arrived at the camp, but the prisoners very often did not receive these shipments. One prisoner at the camp in Elmira, New York, wrote that "unless we were in the hospital, or could furnish a certificate of sickness, the ham, cheese, bread and pie were put back in the wagon and hauled out to fill other stomachs."

Circular No. 4 also prohibited the distribution of clothing sent by family and friends to prisoners, with the exception of those men who were in prison hospitals. As a result, those men who had been captured on Southern battlefields found themselves without adequate clothing to endure Northern winters. Eventually, the quartermaster of Elmira got permission from Hoffman to distribute clothing, but that clothing was gray or a mixture of gray in color. Clothing of any other color was burned.

Although this order applied to all Northern prison camps, the situation at Elmira was particularly bad, thus earning it the nickname "Hellmira." The 40-acre (16-hectare) camp had been built for five thousand men. As summer ended, the population was seriously overcrowded at just under ten thousand. The camp had not enough barracks or tents to house the men. As was the case on Belle Isle and inside the Andersonville stockade, hundreds of prisoners were forced to live without proper shelter. A large pond within the Elmira camp had become polluted from human wastes and had become a source of disease. With further reduced rations, prisoners trapped and killed rats for additional food.

As of September 21, 1864, the Confederacy and the United States were still "in a perfect standstill on the question of exchanging." Once again, the Confederacy had used the rumor of exchange to prevent prisoners from fleeing the boxcars while being transported from Andersonville to other prisons in Georgia and the Carolinas. Thousands were penned in a stockade in Florence, South Carolina. Many men who had survived Andersonville would die in these camps. Though seriously ill, Ransom was fortunate. In Savannah, Georgia, Confederate guards forced Battese to leave Ransom behind. Battese lay his friend on the pavement near the train with other prisoners too ill to continue the journey. Before Battese left, Ransom gave him the first two books of the diary for safekeeping. If Ransom should die, he hoped the books would survive.

But Ransom did not die. Confederate soldiers took him to a military hospital in Savannah. Although he was still a prisoner of war, the care he received in that hospital saved his life.

Not until late October did the United States and the Confederacy agree to a first step toward a general exchange. That first step was to send relief—food, medical supplies, and clothing—to Union prisoners in Confederate camps. The Union also allowed the Confederacy to purchase supplies from foreign countries. The *New York Times* called the plan "a grand victory for humanity."

Not until mid-November did the Union agent agree to the Confederacy's request to return all sick prisoners regardless of whether or not the Confederacy agreed to a like exchange. In late November, the first Union ships under flags of truce arrived in Southern seaports. Aboard one such ship was a reporter for the *New York Times*. He watched as a Confederate ship moored in the middle of the Savannah

This drawing shows men recently released from Confederate prisons celebrating aboard the Union transport *Eliza Hancox* in November 1864.

River alongside the Union vessel. After agents for both governments exchanged the prisoner rolls (a list of names), the transfer began. First aboard the Union ship were those who could still walk. Many more followed on crutches. The last to board were those carried on stretchers. Once the rebel steamers moved away and the men realized they were, at last, exchanged, a great cheering began.

Once bathed and issued new clothing, the men ate. Barrels of coffee were ready for those who had longed for months for just such a hot drink. Some men shared their thoughts with the reporter. "The prisoners very generally believe that they have been abandoned by our government," the reporter stated in his article. He added, however, that the Confederacy had seeded this idea in the minds of its prisoners. The reporter reminded his readers that many thousands of Union soldiers still languished in prison pens. The exchange had begun but was not yet complete.

Thousands of sick prisoners remained in Andersonville that autumn and winter of 1864. Wirz could be counted among the sick as well. In early September, he had returned to his duties, but he still could not ride his mare. An ambulance brought him to and from camp. Nor could he stand for long periods. He had overseen the transfer of prisoners by sitting in a chair. Frequently during the day, when he could no longer sit upright at his desk, he lay on the cot he had placed in his office. He and the quartermaster, Captain Winder, continued to request supplies—blankets, food, and wood for the barracks. As always, they continued to wait for what the Confederacy could not—or would not—give them.

Confederate lieutenant general Richard Taylor was the son of U.S. president Zachary Taylor.

In November 1864, a train stopped at Andersonville to take on water. Aboard were Confederate troops and a high-ranking officer, Lieutenant General Richard Taylor. Wirz did not know Taylor personally, but he understood the power of rank. Wirz had little rank. His requests for necessary supplies had been ignored by his superior officers. Wirz boarded the train carrying a fistful of supply orders he had placed over the past weeks.

The general listened while Wirz complained of the situation at Andersonville and his inability to secure what the camp desperately needed. "He . . . said that the prisoners were suffering from cold, were destitute of blankets and that he had not wagons to supply fuel," the general wrote. Wirz showed the requisitions he had submitted and asked for his superior officer's assistance. The signature of a general just might bring the relief the camp desperately needed.

The general endorsed the requisitions "in the strongest terms possible, hoping to accomplish some good."

The train whistle sounded. Wirz departed with his documents.

PART II: THE COURT-MARTIAL

MAY 1865 TO NOVEMBER 1865

Macon Ga May 17th 1865

General

I have the honor to report that I have arrested Capt H. Wirz C. S. A.[Confederate States of America} notorious as Commandant of the Andersonville Prison; . . . I respectfully request that this miscreant be brought before a General Court Martial in Washington D. C. Where the evidence in his case can be most readily obtained.

I am Very Respectfully

Your obedient Servant

General J. H. Wilson

Brevet Maj. Genl., Comdg Cav Corps, M.D.M.
[Brevet is a distinction of rank made for gallantry]

CHAPTER EIGHT
THE FIEND

*It is extremely humiliating to be held in prison in mana-
cles [handcuffs], but much more so to be held up to your
countrymen as a demon, accused of charges of which you
are not guilty.*

—RICHARD WINDER, FORMER QUARTERMASTER
OF ANDERSONVILLE PRISON, AUGUST 30, 1865

Sunday morning, April 2, 1865, dawned bright and beautiful. But
in Richmond, John B. Jones, the Confederate clerk employed by
the War Department, was uneasy. The previous day, the Confederate army had engaged in intense fighting in Petersburg, Virginia.
This morning the absence of military dispatches suggested to Jones
an emergency. At two that afternoon, Jones reported that the excite-
ment in the city pervaded the churches. President Davis was attending services at Saint Paul's Church when he received a telegram from
General Lee. No one within the church at the time knew the content
of that telegram, but the president left immediately upon reading it.
Jones would later learn that Lee had sent word to the president that
Petersburg had fallen and he was to evacuate Richmond by nightfall.
Lee's troops were in retreat. They could no longer defend the Confederate capital.

That afternoon Jones observed families lifting trunks into carriages
and riding out of the city. James Seddon, the Confederate secretary of
war, intended to leave Richmond at six in the evening. Jones assumed
that the president and his cabinet (advisers) would flee Richmond at
that time, as well. That evening Jones wrote in his diary: "All is yet

As Confederate officials and soldiers fled Richmond at the end of the Civil War, they were ordered to destroy bridges and set fire to warehouses as they left. The fires raged out of control and destroyed large sections of the city, as shown in this 1865 photograph.

quiet. No explosion, no conflagration [fire], no riots, etc. How long will this continue? When will the enemy come?"

About 100 miles (161 km) separate Richmond, Virginia, then the capital of the Confederacy, from Washington, D.C., the capital of the United States. In 1861 the battle cry of the Union had been "On to Richmond!" Not until the morning of April 3, 1865, however, did the Union actually march into the city. A terrific explosion woke Jones early that morning. The magazine (warehouse) where ammunition was stored had been set aflame. Government warehouses, too, were burning. Jones stood on Capitol Square and watched Union troops, among them regiments of African American soldiers, marching by. The white citizens of Richmond, wrote Jones, were "annoyed that the city should be held mostly by Negro troops."

On April 9, 1865, in the town of Appomattox, Virginia, Confederate general Robert E. Lee *(left at table)* officially surrendered the Army of Northern Virginia to General Ulysses S. Grant *(seated, center right)*.

Within the next two weeks, a sequence of major events occurred like dominoes falling. On April 9, in a house at Appomattox in the Virginia countryside, Lee formally surrendered the Army of Northern Virginia to Grant. Five days later, in Washington, D.C., a Southern actor named John Wilkes Booth stepped into President Lincoln's viewing box during a theater performance, pointed his gun at Lincoln's head, and fired. The president died hours later. In the madness and national grief of the next weeks, a conspiracy theory developed. According to this theory, John Wilkes Booth had plotted the assassination with others, and the plot itself had the approval of Jefferson Davis.

✦━◗ ◖━✦

On May 2, 1865, Captain Henry Noyes was en route to Alabama. Noyes was the aide-de-camp to General James. H. Wilson, who was the Union officer in command of troops in Georgia. The train on which Noyes traveled stopped to take on water and wood at Anderson

On April 14, 1865, actor John Wilkes Booth assassinated President Lincoln while he was attending a performance at the Ford Theater.

Station. Noyes stepped down from his car to stretch his legs and look around. Nearby, he spied a number of Union prisoners, so weak they could not stand without the help of a fellow soldier.

A few men in Confederate uniforms were urging the sick prisoners to sign papers for parole, or release. Noyes turned away and boarded the train. Through the open window, he heard one man threaten the prisoners, "Hurry up and sign these paroles or you'll die here anyhow." Angered at this poor treatment of Union soldiers, Noyes stood, intending to put an end to it. Just then the cars jerked forward. Through the window, Noyes saw Wirz standing among the prisoners.

When he returned to Macon, Noyes reported to General Wilson that the commandant of Andersonville had not fled the camp, as other Confederate officers had done. Wilson ordered Noyes to return to Andersonville and arrest the commandant. The general ordered another officer to the camp to seize all prison documents.

A few days later, Noyes once again stepped off a train onto the platform of Anderson Station. He found Wirz in his home with his wife and daughters. He asked Wirz to accompany him to Macon for an interview with General Wilson. At once, Wirz's wife objected. She feared that the U.S. government intended to hang her husband as a traitor to the Union. She and her children began to cry. Wirz, too, became quite agitated. Was he not protected under the terms of surrender signed by Grant and Lee at Appomattox, terms that provided amnesty (freedom from prosecution) for Confederate soldiers and their leaders?

"It is a very hard thing to take a man from his family," Noyes would later state. Still, Noyes had his orders. He attempted to calm the wife and children. If Wirz had done no more than his duty, he had nothing to fear. If his actions were the result of orders given to him by his superior officers, then very likely Wilson would detain him no longer than a day. Wirz interpreted Noyes's words to be a promise of safe return. Under this unwritten promise, he agreed to cooperate. He dressed in his Confederate uniform and proceeded to the train depot with Noyes and his Union guard.

While waiting for the train, Wirz wrote a letter to Wilson. Under the terms of surrender agreed to by both the Union and the Confederacy, Wirz believed he was protected from any prosecution. In this letter, he asked for the general's promise of amnesty. As commandant of the interior of the prison, Wirz explained, he was not accountable for the lack of clothing or food or the overcrowded conditions at Andersonville. He was "the tool in the hands" of his superiors. "The duties I had to perform were arduous [difficult] and unpleasant, and I am satisfied that no man can or will justly blame me for things that happened here, and which were beyond my power to control," he wrote.

The letter continued. He was a man with a family, a man who had lost everything—his home and his health. He had no money and no place to go. His life was in danger, for the prisoners sought vengeance upon him. If the general could give him safe conduct, he wrote, his intention was to take his family and return to his native Switzerland.

In Macon, Wirz remained under guard in a prison. Noyes reported to Wilson that he had returned with the prisoner. The family had cried, Noyes added. The tears of one man's family were not the general's concern, however.

In his prison cell, Wirz waited for Wilson to summon him. But the general refused to see him, and Wirz's letter went unanswered. No matter what Noyes might have suggested to the commandant or the words Wirz had penned in his letter, Wilson had no intention of releasing his prisoner.

One week after Wirz's arrest, on May 14, 1865, Secretary of War Stanton received this official communication from Lieutenant Colonel B. D. Pritchard in Georgia: "Sir; I have the honor to report that at daylight yesterday, at Irwinsville I surprised and captured Jeff[erson] Davis and family."

With the arrest of the former president of the Confederacy, the Union's wheels of justice—though many would call it vengeance—began to roll. In the months ahead, the following Confederate officers associated with Andersonville would also be arrested: Quartermaster Captain Richard

Jefferson Davis, the president of the former Confederate States of America, was arrested on May 10, 1865, by the Union army. He remained in military custody at Fortress Monroe, Virginia, until May 14, 1867, when he was released on a bond of one hundred thousand dollars.

Winder, surgeon Isaiah White, and Robert Ould, the Confederate commissioner of prisoner exchange. Fate, however, had spared General John Winder. On February 6, 1865, soon after entering the prison compound at Florence, South Carolina, the general suffered a fatal heart attack. Had the general lived, perhaps history would have written a very different next chapter for Andersonville and for Wirz.

⟶ ══◦═ ⟵

On May 20, 1865, Noyes left Macon, Georgia, for Washington, D.C., with Wirz in custody. The commandant still wore his Confederate uniform. Word of his journey seemed to travel faster than the train on which he and Noyes were riding. At depot stops along the route, crowds gathered—some to see but most to curse the Andersonville jailer.

In Chattanooga, Tennessee, Noyes sent Wirz under guard to the prison at a nearby military camp for the duration of the stop. When Noyes saw Wirz again, he was shocked by his appearance. "His clothes were stripped off him; he had only part of his hat, no coat, a dirty shirt, and a portion of a pair of pants pretty badly torn," Noyes stated. The soldiers at the post had attacked him. Although these men had not been imprisoned in Andersonville, they had heard stories of intentional starvation. They handed out their own brand of justice on behalf of their fellow bluecoats.

In Nashville, too, Noyes had difficulty getting Wirz onto the train, so violent was the abuse by the soldiers at the depot. Noyes began to worry that he would not be able to deliver his prisoner alive. At Louisville, Kentucky, Wirz had acquaintances that could help him. Noyes agreed to a disguise. With Noyes's help, Wirz secured a black suit and a beaver hat. He shaved his beard. Shaving, perhaps more than any article of clothing, changed the man's appearance. The remainder of the journey northward was mostly uneventful.

In Washington, D.C., the government confined Wirz to a room in the Old Capitol Prison. Secretary of War Stanton ordered a special military commission to look into what were called war crimes at Andersonville. He ordered Lieutenant Colonel Norton P. Chipman to serve as the prosecuting attorney responsible for bringing the U.S. government's case against Wirz to trial and convicting him.

Chipman adamantly believed that the South must pay for its crime of withdrawing from the United States, which had cost the nation so many thousands of lives. Chipman was also ambitious. The trial of the

After serving as the prosecutor in the Wirz trial, Norton P. Chipman published his recollections of the famous proceedings in his 1911 book, *The Tragedy of Andersonville*.

Andersonville jailer was sure to be highly publicized. Convicting Wirz could only advance Chipman's career. He began his investigation enthusiastically. Preparation to go to trial would take three months. The military commission that was set up to prepare the case interviewed not only Andersonville survivors but also doctors and former Confederate officers associated with the prison. "It was known that the mortality had been great," Chipman would later state. But no one, he said, not even the prisoners inside the stockade, knew that the number of dead was nearly thirteen thousand men.

In fact, one person did know exactly how many had died and who they were: Dorence Atwater.

It was during Wirz's absence from Andersonville that prisoner Dorence Atwater began a secret mission. Atwater had been sixteen when he volunteered to fight in the War of Rebellion. Like many youths of the time, Atwater lied about his age to enlist. Tall and slender, with long sideburns over his jaw, he was an expert horseman. In Hartford, Connecticut, he mustered, or enrolled into military service, with the 2nd Regiment, which would be known as the Harris Light Cavalry.

The Union army recognized in Atwater a youth who was both courageous and educated. His penmanship was particularly neat. Many of Atwater's assignments were to carry important documents from one camp to another, delivering them to the officers in command. He also participated in foraging raids in and around Richmond. In the days immediately following the 1863 Battle of Gettysburg in Pennsylvania, Atwater accompanied the Harris Light Cavalry into Maryland in pursuit of retreating Confederate forces. On Tuesday morning, July 7, 1863, Confederate soldiers took him prisoner. Along with other bluecoats captured during the bloody fighting at Gettysburg, Atwater marched south into Virginia. He spent months in a cotton warehouse, where the Confederacy made good use of Atwater's clerking and penmanship skills. He kept an account of the supplies received from the United States

If anyone could be called a hero in the tragic story of Andersonville, it would be Dorence Atwater, who quietly labored at the self-assigned task of keeping a record of the thirteen thousand soldiers who died at Andersonville.

for distribution to the prisoners. Working inside the warehouse might well have saved Atwater's life that winter, while other captives on Belle Isle died from exposure. In February 1864, Atwater was among the first group of prisoners removed from Richmond for Camp Sumter, Georgia.

For three months, Atwater had survived inside the stockade. Just how he came to the attention of Wirz is not known for certain. On June 15, 1864, Dorence Atwater received a furlough to work outside the stockade as a clerk in Wirz's headquarters under the supervision of Confederate surgeon Isaiah H. White. The gaunt young man of nineteen sat at a desk. His daily task was to record the names of the dead and their regiments. The numbers appalled him. He struggled to make sense of why so many men were dying of dysentery, scurvy, and typhus.

As the death rate soared with the blistering heat that August, Atwater began to suspect that perhaps his jailers were intentionally starving the prisoners. Their motivation, he believed, was to ensure that the prisoners were unfit for further military service should the prisoner exchanges ever take place. Atwater felt compelled to do something.

Atwater believed that if Union troops rescued the men inside the stockade, General Winder would order the camp's records destroyed. And so Atwater secretly began to copy the entire list of men who had died at Andersonville. In addition to their names, he recorded their company and regiment, cause of death, date of death, and grave number. If a rebel soldier discovered the document, Atwater was certain to face severe punishment. Nevertheless, Atwater took the risk. Week after week, month after month, Atwater's list of names grew longer.

Atwater had survived Andersonville. He was emaciated, as most Andersonville prisoners were, when he was exchanged in March 1865. Once back on Union soil, he wrote to Secretary of War Stanton. He told the war secretary that he was in possession of a death register, which he had copied while at Andersonville and smuggled out of the prison. He wished to publish it to relieve the many thousands of "anxious families" who had no knowledge of what had happened to their sons, fathers, and husbands. On April 12, 1865, just days after Lee had surrendered to Grant at Appomattox, Atwater received a telegram from the War Department. His orders were to report to Washington at once to deliver his roll of names. Not yet fully recovered from his imprisonment and a bout with diphtheria, Atwater at once delivered the rolls to the officer in charge.

In exchange for the names, the U.S. government offered to pay Atwater three hundred dollars for the death register. He refused. The rolls of names were not for sale. He wanted no money. In reply, the officer told him that the government would confiscate the register rather than have it sold for profit. Again, Atwater insisted he had no intention of using the names for profit. He only wanted to help families learn the truth about their men. Then Atwater suggested an alternative. Perhaps the government would give him a clerkship so that he could copy the rolls and then keep the originals. The government agreed, with one stipulation: Atwater had to reenlist in military service.

At this same time, a woman named Clara Barton was already serving a clerkship with the U.S. government. During the war, Barton had received a general pass to travel with army ambulances, distributing medical supplies and nursing the wounded. Although the war had ended, her work on behalf of the soldiers and their families had not. The War Department had given her an official, if not concise, title: General Correspondent for the Friends of Paroled Prisoners.

According to the government's estimate at the time, the number of Union soldiers buried during four years of war exceeded 315,000. But the identities of the men in at least half of those graves were unknown. Grieving families had learned that their men had died, but they did not know where they had been buried. In addition, thousands of men were listed as missing. In June 1865, the *New York Times* published a brief

Although best remembered for her nursing skills during the Civil War and as the founder of the American Red Cross, Clara Barton played a major role in creating the cemetery at Andersonville.

message from Barton, asking families to contact her with the names and regiments of soldiers who were missing or reported dead and whose graves remained unknown. She would attempt to locate the information. Letters arrived by the hundreds from all across the country.

Atwater had been praying for this opportunity. He contacted Barton immediately, telling her he could help her identify the graves of nearly thirteen thousand prisoners of war who had died at Andersonville. From her first encounter with Atwater, Barton was impressed by his intelligence and his frankness. Within weeks the two were on a train riding south to Georgia. With them were Captain J. P. Moore and forty-two painters and clerks to erect and print names on grave markers. Stanton had approved the mission, assigning Moore as the project's official Union officer. Barton praised Stanton's decision, assuring him that the American people would "bless" him for his "humane" act.

On the afternoon of July 25, 1865, Atwater once again stood before the gates of the Andersonville stockade. A little more than a year before, he had stood in this same spot as a fresh fish. Now he was free. Whatever his thoughts were at that moment, he never said. Beside him stood Barton, who would later write, "Andersonville was not the gateway to hell; it was hell itself."

Inside, the camp had not changed significantly. The lone cabin, the sutler's store, still stood, as did the deadline. The remnants of shebangs—tattered pieces of blanket and pine sticks—littered the hillsides. The water wells and the burrows remained. Barton walked the acres inside the pen and imagined the men who had crawled into those holes to escape the sun and rain. She peered into the burrows and found the moldy remnants of food, "drinking cups made of sections of horns, platters and spoons wrought from parts of old canteens."

Each man had a mother, and many had wives. They had been loved by someone. "I thought of the widows . . . ," she would later write, "north and south, from the pine [the North] to the palm [the South], the shadows on the hearths and hearts over all my country—sore, broken hearts; ruined, desolate homes."

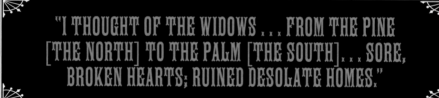

"I THOUGHT OF THE WIDOWS . . . FROM THE PINE [THE NORTH] TO THE PALM [THE SOUTH] . . . SORE, BROKEN HEARTS; RUINED DESOLATE HOMES."

The camp's cemetery was 300 yards (274 m) from the stockade. Under Wilson's orders, both the camp and its cemetery had been protected. In some places, heavy rains had washed away the soil over the burial trenches. In other instances, wild animals had rooted in the earth and disturbed the gravesites. Wilson's troops had maintained the graves, adding soil and reburying bodies when necessary.

With the arrival of Atwater and Barton, the work of identifying the graves began. Moore's crew of workers constructed a fence to enclose the 50-acre (20-hectare) cemetery. They built and erected a 2-foot-high (0.6 m) tablet at the head of each grave. In black lettering against a painted white background appeared the name, company, and regiment of the soldier buried beneath. The men had been buried so closely, side by side, that the tablets were nearly touching one another. Within just a few weeks, Barton and Atwater were able to identify all but about four hundred graves. These the painters marked as "unknown."

The work crew and their leaders had worked tirelessly, often long into the night. One night in August, when their mission was almost complete, Barton found Atwater alone in the cemetery. Exhausted, he had broken down at last. She led him back to his tent. Throughout the night, she sat beside him as she had sat beside and consoled so many wounded soldiers on the battlefield. Atwater's wounds were not physical. They were deep inside him. By morning he had recovered his composure, but the emotional wounds of Andersonville would stay with him forever.

The Andersonville cemetery as originally restored by Atwater and Barton is a national cemetery maintained by the U.S. National Park Service at the Andersonville National Historic Site.

This illustration from *Harper's Weekly* shows Clara Barton in the far background raising the U.S. flag among the graves at Andersonville in 1865.

On August 17, less than three weeks after the team had arrived in Andersonville, Moore held a dedication ceremony for the cemetery. Barton had the honor of raising the U.S. flag in the cemetery. Then it was Clara Barton who was overcome with emotion. That day she would write in her diary about the Stars and Stripes, "Up and there it drooped as if in grief and sadness, till at length the sunlight streamed out its beautiful folds—the men struck up the Star Spangled Banner, and I covered my face and wept."

＊＝◎＝＊

While Atwater and Barton were completing their work at the cemetery in Andersonville, Chipman had been busy. He identified individuals associated with the prison pen and issued subpoenas, a formal order requiring them to give testimony at Wirz's trial. In the Old Capital Prison, Wirz's health was failing once again. His bandaged arm reeked of gangrene. His wife and daughters had come to Washington, but the War Department refused to let them visit him. Wirz was bewildered by his imprisonment. He did not know why he, of all the officers associated with Andersonville, had been arrested. He couldn't believe that the U.S. government would hold him responsible for the faults of the commissary and quartermaster departments over which he had no control.

He longed to return home to Switzerland with his wife and daughters. His fate, however, was in the hands of two young men, Louis Schade and Orrin Baker, the attorneys who had agreed to defend him. Wirz had no money to pay for their services. Even so, the attorneys believed that the U.S. government was using him as a scapegoat, intending to punish him for the sins committed by the Confederacy itself. This was why Schade and Baker took the case. Wirz had given the men a list of individuals who he was certain could testify on his behalf.

Defending Wirz was not going to be easy. Wirz's name appeared frequently, if not daily, in newspapers as the start date for the trial neared. The *New York Times* labeled him "devil" and "An Incarnate Fiend."[104] It published "evidence" of Wirz's barbarity, quoting a former prisoner from Illinois. Men were shot for crossing the deadline, even when just reaching for water, the soldier told the *New York Times* reporter. He went on to tell how, when the men shouted to Wirz for more bread, the commandant answered that he didn't "pack bread." He "packed bullets" for Yankees. Perhaps most sensational of all were the images. In June 1864, *Harper's Weekly* had published photographs of severely emaciated prisoners.

Wirz's attorneys asked the press to refrain from judgment until the trial had been held. The attorneys did not deny that atrocities had occurred. But they said that the guilty person was not necessarily Wirz. The *New York Times* responded by suggesting that the defense attorneys were "demented." No one would believe that Wirz was just following orders of superior officers. And even if he were, the editors continued, why did he not protest? No one, not even a superior officer, could force a man to treat other human beings with such "deviltry" as forced starvation.

The trial had not yet begun, but the press had already convicted Wirz.

LETTERS TO CLARA BARTON

GRATITUDE OF A BROKEN-HEARTED MOTHER

Paw Paw, Van Buren Co., Michigan,

July the 5th, 1865.

Dear Madam: — Seeing a notice in the paper of the effort you are making to ascertain [discover] the fate of missing soldiers from Michigan, I hasten to address you in regard to my son. His name is Eugene P. Osborne. He was a private in the 13th Michigan Regiment, Co. H Infantry; was in Sherman's Army; left Atlanta last November with the Regiment, became lame soon after leaving there, and fell out the first day of December, near Louisville, Georgia. Since that time we have never been able to learn anything of him, or what has become of him. Those that went with him from this place, and were in the Company with him, have returned, but they know not what has become of him, or what his fate may be. We have endeavored to learn something of him by writing to various persons and places, but as yet we have heard nothing reliable. Will you, Oh! will you, aid me in the search for

Before taking action on behalf of the victims of Andersonville, Clara Barton had obtained permission to travel behind enemy lines to deliver supplies and to nurse wounded soldiers.

my loved but unfortunate son; if so, the prayers and gratitude of a heart-broken Mother shall be yours. Please answer without delay and tell me if you know aught [anything] concerning him, for this cruel suspense is dreadful.

Respectfully yours,

Mrs. C. A. OSBORNE

Dear Angel of Love and Mercy:

I address these few lines to you hoping to get some information in regard to my son's remains. He died in August in the dreadful prison pen at Andersonville. I think it was about the ninth day of the month. Did you find when you were there on the list the name of Edward H. Walton, Co. H, 57th Regt. Massachusetts Volunteers? If so, you will confer a great kindness on me, his poor heartbroken Mother, by giving me what information you can. He went from Worcester, Mass.

Please let me know if you think I could obtain his remains if I should send for them, as I am very anxious to get them. I shall ever remember your great kindness and labor in thus giving me the comfort that you have seen the remains of the poor murdered ones decently buried. I thank you from my very heart and may heaven bless you while you live and when you have done on earth may the richest of heaven's blessings be yours through that never ending eternity for which thousands of mothers will pray.

Mrs. Dolly Walton,

Worcester, MA

Mother of Edward H. Walton, Co. H, Fifty- seventh Regt. Mass. Vol.,

died at Andersonville Prison in August, '64.

CHAPTER NINE
FACTS AND FABRICATIONS

*Wirz puts in a plea, if true, will shield him from the pun-
ishment he so dreads. He asserts that the suffering of our
prisoners was not inflicted by him—that they were unavoidable, that the rebel government could not give them
more food, or better shelter, or more kindly treatment
than it did. This is just what the present trial is to test.*

"WIRZ AND THE UNION PRISONERS,"
NEW YORK TIMES, AUGUST 31, 1865

On Monday, August 21, 1865, in the Court of Claims room in the
U.S. Capitol in Washington, D.C., Henry Wirz faced his accusers.
The court included three generals, three brigadier generals, and
three lieutenant colonels. All had commanded on Union battlefields.
On that morning, each was in "dress uniform and gleaming brass."
When Wirz entered the courtroom surrounded by eight guards, every-
one turned to stare. For many, this was the first time they had seen
the prisoner.

Overseeing the military tribunal was Major General Lew Wallace.
Wallace dreaded staying in Washington during the hot summer
months. The nation's capital, lying on the banks of the Potomac
River, was a notorious breeding ground for mosquitoes. Earlier
that summer, Wallace had served on the commission that tried the
people involved in the assassination of President Abraham Lincoln. His experience with that trial, as well as his understanding
of law, seemingly was the reason he had been appointed to pre-
side over the Wirz Commission. He referred to his appointment as

"this onerous [burdensome] duty." He would have much preferred to be at home with his wife, revising the book he was writing on military tactics.

In a letter, Wallace described his first impression of the jailer of Andersonville. "Wirz is a singular [unique] looking genius. He has a small head, retreating forehead . . . the hair, light in color, is very thin . . . prominent ears, small, sharp pointed nose, moustache and beard heavy enough to conceal the mouth and lower face, and of the dirty tobacco-stained color, eyes large, and of mixed blue and gray, very restless and reminding you continually of a cat's when the animal is excited by the scent of prey."

A. J. Riddle photographed Henry Wirz *(above)* during his August 1864 visit to Andersonville.

The charges were read. The first charge stated that Wirz had "maliciously [with evil intent], willfully, and traitorously" conspired "to injure the health and destroy the lives of soldiers in the military service of the United States." The second charge included thirteen counts of murder. Each murder specification provided not only the date of the murder but also the manner in which the murder had been perpetrated—beatings and gunshots, for example. The specifications did not list the names of the thirteen victims, however. In each instance, the victim was identified by the phrase *a prisoner of war, whose name is unknown.* The court called for the defendant (the person on trial, Wirz) to plead to the charges.

Wirz's attorney, Louis Schade, played his first card of defense. He moved to have the trial dismissed on the grounds that Wirz had been protected by the amnesty terms of Lee's surrender. Having asked for amnesty, Wirz had gone willingly to Macon, Georgia, with Noyes on May 7, 1865. He believed Noyes had made him that promise. After some deliberation, Wallace denied the motion.

Schade was prepared. His next move was to ask that the charges be dismissed on the grounds that Wirz was no longer a soldier but a civilian. As such, he had the right to a trial by a jury of his peers and not by a military tribunal. Again, Wallace denied the motion. Finally, Schade asked the court for additional days to prepare the case, claiming that he had not known the specifics of the charges until this morning. This, too, the court denied.

Once again the court asked the defendant to plead to the charges. Schade answered for Wirz. Not guilty.

Later, as the guards escorted Wirz from the courtroom, the crowd waiting outside pressed forward. "How are you, Wirz?" a soldier shouted, as if he knew the commandant. Wirz recoiled from the rush of the crowd. The guards quickly cleared a path to move their prisoner safely from the building.

And so the trial of the Andersonville jailer began.

⸎

Day after day, as witnesses took the stand, Wirz sat with legs crossed and listened intently. He held his right hand to his mouth and nervously tugged at his beard. Day after day, the press reported on the testimony. The reporters' depictions of Wirz were critical and biased. A reporter for the *Philadelphia Inquirer* thought Wirz's black coat and trousers "seedy-looking" and the man himself "nervous, agitated." A correspondent for the *Boston Daily Advertiser* wrote that Wirz was "scorned, loathed, despised, and hated by all men and women. . . . One almost wondered that there was no outraged soldier to take the law into his own hands and shoot the miserable creature as he walked with his guard."

The prosecution called Noyes to testify. Chipman showed him a letter supposedly written by Wirz on May 7, 1865. Yes, Noyes stated, he knew of the letter. It was the same letter Wirz had written the day Noyes had escorted him from Andersonville to Wilson's headquarters in Macon. Wirz's attorneys had claimed the letter was evidence that the commandant had asked Wilson for protection. Noyes testified that he never promised Wirz amnesty.

Lieutenant Colonel Persons, formerly of the Confederacy, gave testimony on behalf of the defense. "I know that Captain Wirz objected to the prison being overcrowded as it was. We sent an objection to the authorities at Richmond, to General Winder, and urged him to hold up and not to ship any more there; but he [Winder] paid no attention to it." Persons stated too that the order to use dogs to capture escaped prisoners had also come from General Winder. As it was an order, Wirz had to obey.

When pressed by Chipman, Persons admitted, "I cannot say that Captain Wirz did all that it was in his power to do to alleviate [lessen] the sufferings of the prisoners. I know he labored indefatigably [tirelessly], but whether he accomplished everything he might have accomplished, of course I cannot say. All I know is that the prison was not half cared for. I know that very well."

Next, the prosecution called Dr. John Bates, a Confederate surgeon who had served at Andersonville. Bates described the patients in the hospital as "destitute [utterly lacking]" of clothing and bedding. The doctors had no medicine. There wasn't enough wood to build fires to warm the men, and he had seen cases of frostbite. The patients had little protection from the rain.

Baker, representing Wirz, objected. The doctor's testimony had nothing to do with the defendant, as he was responsible only for the interior of the prison and not the exterior, where the hospital was located. The court overruled the objection. Bates's testimony continued.

The diet was monotonous, he said, consisting of cornmeal and peas, often of poor quality, and occasionally sweet potatoes. Beef, too, was occasionally issued. Sometimes the beef was good, and sometimes it was rancid. Such a monotonous diet for a long period of time would result in illness. "It is my opinion that men starved to death," the doctor stated.

Dr. John Jones, also formerly of the Confederacy, testified. He had not arrived at Andersonville until September, and he had come purposely to study the symptoms of disease prevalent in the camp. The high mortality rate was not due to climate, soil, or foul water, he explained. The accumulation of filth and human wastes compromised,

The Washington, D.C., trial of Captain Henry Wirz was fraught with drama as witness after witness described the horrors of what went on inside the Andersonville stockade.

or weakened, the men's health. As a result, gangrene was rampant in the hospital. But ultimately, scurvy and the complications caused by that disease killed thousands. Scurvy could have been prevented through proper diet.

The attorney for the defense attempted to enter into evidence a letter written by Wirz to his superior officers. Wirz had complained of the poor quality of the rations. The court denied the admission of this evidence, however, on the grounds that the prisoner could not speak in his own defense in a military tribunal.

Round and round the questioning went. Witnesses for the prosecution were cross-examined by the counsel for the defense. Witnesses for the defense were cross-examined by the prosecution. Wallace overruled most of the objections made by the defense. Wirz's attorneys became so frustrated with evidence denied and objections overruled that they told the court they wished to quit the case.

Wirz pleaded with his attorneys not to abandon him. If they left the courtroom, his fate would be left totally in the hands of the prosecutor. Schade and Baker relented. The trial continued.

⋆⇒◉⇐⋆

Robert Kellogg was among the first of the former Andersonville inmates to give testimony. He did not speak of the day when Wirz had allowed him to return to the woods to retrieve his much-needed pocket knife. Rather, guided by questions from Chipman, Kellogg shared his knowledge of the deadline. "I have seen the penalty enforced—I have seen sentries shoot," he stated. He told of a crippled, one-legged man who had been shot. Under cross-examination, he admitted he had not actually seen the cripple shot. And the man had not been dead when he was carried away from the stockade.

BORED ON THE BENCH

A parade of witnesses at Wirz's trial provided gruesome details of inhumane treatment as a result of Wirz's command. Ferocious, bloodthirsty hounds tore to pieces numerous prisoners who had escaped into the nearby pines or swamp. Wirz had set the dogs upon them, they said. Wirz punished those who had attempted escape by placing them in stockades, stringing them up by the thumbs, putting them in irons with heavy iron balls, or refusing them water or rations. In the hospital, the surgeons had vaccinated the prisoners for smallpox using poison that had resulted in sores that became gangrenous. Maggots swarmed in the open wounds of the sick.

And yet, for all those graphic details, the trial not only bored Lew Wallace but actually irritated him. As he had expected, Wirz's defense strategy amounted to nothing more than claiming Wirz had just been following orders. Wallace was particularly annoyed by "the dullest, most pointless cross-examinations" of witnesses.

While the testimony proceeded, Wallace made a sketch of a man in a faded blue uniform lying on the ground. In his outstretched hand, he held a cup. He had been reaching for water. The image excited him, the general told his wife. He planned to paint it on canvas. He thought his rendition was rather good.

Wirz trial judge Major General Lew Wallace was a man of many talents. After the war, he became the territorial governor of New Mexico, served as ambassador to the Ottoman Empire, and wrote the novel *Ben-Hur*.

"I came near to being shot once myself," Kellogg continued. On May 5, 1864, two days after arriving, he had sat at the side of the stream but was too close to the deadline. He heard a shot. A sentry had fired at him, "but the piece had missed."

Other inmates told similar stories—hearsay of men shot and killed by Wirz. But no one, not even Robert Kellogg, could provide the names of those men. Horatio B. Terrell, of Ohio, swore that a prisoner had approached Wirz one day and showed him his scant ration of corn and asked for more. Wirz pulled his revolver and cursed, "I'll give you bullets for bread."

In what hand was he holding the gun? counsel asked. Terrell presumed it was his right hand.

Terrell knew of another incident. Wirz shot a black soldier in the back. Terrell had seen the body and the wound. Under cross-examination, he admitted he had not actually seen the captain shoot him. It was something he had heard about. When asked why the soldier had been shot, Terrell presumed he had rolled under the deadline.

Was Terrell aware of the rules regarding the deadline, that crossing the deadline would result in being shot? Yes, Terrell said. He was.

On September 12, Felix DeLabaume, of New York, entered the courtroom. He described a disturbing event. His regiment had just arrived at Anderson Station, and the men had fallen in line while Wirz reviewed them. One of the soldiers suffered an epileptic fit. Two soldiers fell out of rank to get water to assist the man. DeLabaume saw Wirz shoot the two men. One of the men was bleeding heavily from the chest, and in DeLabaume's opinion, was "in a dying condition."

James K. Davidson, of Iowa, gave the press a phrase they could print in bold letters. "I have heard Captain Wirz say that he was killing more damned Yankees there than Lee was at Richmond," he stated. "That was in August; he was in my wagon at the time. I had been to the graveyard with the dead men."

⋆⇒◉⇐⋆

Early in September, Wirz wrote to the court, asking for the benefit of a spiritual counselor. He requested that Father Peter Whelan and Father John Hamilton, two Catholic priests whom he had known at Andersonville, be allowed to meet with him in his cell. The War Department denied the request. The government had subpoenaed both priests to testify. Until their testimony had been entered into record, they could not meet privately with Wirz.

A few days later, Wirz was too ill to appear in court. The newspapers reported that he was overcome by nerves and emotion. Each witness who took the stand provided gruesome details about life inside the stockade, and always, they identified Wirz as the man responsible. As the evidence of cruelty mounted against him, Wirz had become more agitated, the *New York Times* stated. When Wirz did not appear in court the following day, the rumor began to circulate that the Andersonville jailer had died.

Wirz's attorneys soon confirmed that their client was terribly weak. He was also despondent and unable to concentrate. He was still without a spiritual adviser. The court ordered a sofa brought into the courtroom so the defendant could be present while the trial continued. The newspapers thought the sofa luxurious, a far cry from the filthy ground on which soldier boys had lain in Andersonville. Still, the guards carried Wirz into the courtroom on a stretcher and transferred him to the sofa. In the days and weeks that followed, Wirz seemed less interested in the proceedings. He often lay on the sofa with a cool cloth over his face. He did not protest any of the testimony or confer with his attorneys as frequently as he had in the past.

The October 21, 1865, issue of *Harper's Weekly* published a sketch of Captain Wirz, too ill to even sit, lying on a couch during his trial.

At last, Father Hamilton was called to testify. When asked to comment on the condition of the camp, the priest provided a graphic example. When he entered the stockade, he was wearing a white linen coat, he said. After perhaps just ten or fifteen minutes, he noticed that vermin covered his coat. He removed it, giving it to a guard to hold. The prosecutors then asked him to comment on the condition of the men. Father Hamilton replied that he was too occupied in performing his duties to observe very much. But he added, "I could not keep my eyes closed as to what I saw there. . . . I saw a great many men perfectly naked," he said. He had frequently crawled on his hands and knees to enter the burrows where dying men were lying to hear their confessions.

The defense cross-examined the witness. When asked if prisoners had complained to him of ill treatment on the part of Wirz, the priest answered no. "I never heard of any prisoner dying from any such treatment from the hands of Captain Wirz, nor from any personal violence from him."

Whelan also testified that Wirz had cared about the men's spiritual needs, shown by his granting the priest permission to enter the stockade daily. During the summer of 1864, Whelan usually went inside the pen at nine in the morning. He often stayed until after four in the afternoon. He had accompanied the six condemned Raiders to the gallows and pleaded for their lives. Although he spent a great deal of time inside the stockade with the men, he, like Hamilton, had been "occupied" with his own business.

"How then could you see and know everything that transpired there in reference to Captain Wirz?" Chipman challenged him.

"I did not say that I did," the priest answered.

"You have said that if he had committed acts of violence you would have known it?"

"I said it was highly probable I should have known it through report."

"Why?" Chipman pressed.

Such acts of violence would have been rumored throughout the camp, the priest explained. "If such a public act as murdering a man there were done, I would have heard of it."

"Did you ever hear anything said there about Captain Wirz being a cruel man?"

"I heard some prisoners saying he was a violent man," Whelan admitted.

"What else did you hear them say about him?"

"Nothing more than that he was a violent man; that he was harsh to some and cursed them."

⋅→⫘⊙⫘←⋅

Earlier in the summer, Wirz had identified individuals to

testify on his behalf. Specifically, he named officers in charge of the commissary, including Quartermaster Richard Winder, to provide evidence that Wirz had had no control over rations or supplies. He also named Robert Ould, the Confederate agent for prisoner exchanges. Ould would testify that the Confederacy had attempted to release sick prisoners in August 1864 and that their requests had remained unanswered by the Union War Department for months.

Yet many of the individuals Wirz had named as witnesses in his defense were difficult to track down. Some, as it turned out, had fled the country to avoid a fate similar to the commandant's. But others willingly

Captain Richard B. Winder *(above)* had been assigned by his second cousin Brigadier General John Winder to design and oversee the building of Camp Sumter as well as to serve as its quartermaster.

stepped forward to speak. When Ould arrived in Washington, Chipman visited him personally and revoked his subpoena. Chipman gave no reason other than Ould's testimony was not needed. This forced Ould to leave the city. Ould was never given the opportunity to testify in Wirz's defense.

James Madison Page, likewise, had received a subpoena. He was quite willing to appear on Wirz's behalf. Wirz was a verbally abusive man, but Page had witnessed his small acts of kindness. The prosecution never called Page to the courtroom. He was "sorely disappointed," for he believed his knowledge of Wirz differed greatly from what he was reading in the newspapers.

One witness for the defense was former prisoner Martin S. Harris of New York. Chipman asked him why he had found it necessary to enter into a defense of Wirz. Harris said he never meant to deny the horrors of Andersonville, but he wanted to ensure that the proper parties were punished. "You do not today deny any of the horrors that have been depicted at Andersonville?"

"No, not a particle," Harris answered.

Wallace interrupted. "On whom, in your opinion, is the responsibility?"

"In my opinion, General Winder was responsible." Then he added, "and also the prisoners themselves, by their conduct toward each other; the prisoners were responsible themselves in a great many cases for their horrible sufferings there."

Chipman found this statement quite difficult to believe. He would later state that Harris had received "favors at the hands of Wirz." His overzealous testimony was in gratitude for those favors.

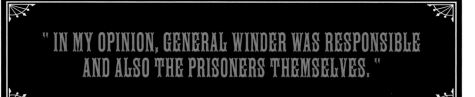

" IN MY OPINION, GENERAL WINDER WAS RESPONSIBLE AND ALSO THE PRISONERS THEMSELVES. "

Edward Wellington Boate was one of the last inmates to testify. "During the time I remained in the stockade, I never knew or heard of Captain Wirz committing any assault on any prisoner there. I never heard of such a thing as Captain Wirz shooting, beating, or in any way injuring a man so that he died," Boate stated, "until this trial."

Boate had been one of the men in the delegation sent to petition President Lincoln for a speedy release of the Andersonville prisoners. The delegation had Wirz's full approval and support. The defense attorney submitted to the court as evidence a copy of the petition the prisoners had drafted for President Lincoln's attention. This document proved that Wirz had gone beyond his limits of power to do a humane act.

Chipman objected. The letter had never been delivered to the president, Chipman surmised. If it had, such an esteemed man as Abraham Lincoln would not have refused to see the prisoners. To accept the letter as evidence was slander on the dead president.

Wallace agreed and sustained the objection. The letter was not put into evidence.

⊷══◉══⊶

From the beginning, Wirz's trial had been a battle of wills and points of law between defense attorneys and the prosecuting attorney. Baker argued that the government's witnesses proved only that men had suffered. But their testimony did not prove that Wirz was responsible for that suffering. Wirz had been ill and away from the camp through most of August, a period when many of the charges of cruelty against him allegedly occurred. The witnesses could not even remember the names of the victims.

"I doubt whether you or I would remember anything if we had gone through what they have," Chipman fired back.

"Then you should not attempt to prove it," Baker said, his frustration obvious in his tone of voice.

Wallace threatened to expel Baker from the courtroom for disrespectful behavior.

In the final days of the trial, the counsel for the defense called two doctors to exam Wirz's arm and shoulder. In the courtroom, the doctors described the prisoner's physical condition. The arm was swollen, inflamed, and ulcerated in three places. "In addition to that, I believe that portions of both bones of the arm are dead," the doctor stated.

The defense attorney asked the doctor to comment on the strength of the arm in its present condition. "Would he be capable with that arm of pushing or knocking down a person, or using any heavy or even a light instrument in doing so?"

"I don't know that I can answer that question entirely," the doctor began. " . . . I should think him incapable of knocking a man, or lifting a very heavy instrument of any kind, without doing great injury to the arm."

The doctor further testified that Wirz's deltoid muscle in his left shoulder was "entirely gone." Only the front portion of the shoulder muscle remained. This, he said, would make lifting the arm impossible.

The wound was old, not new, the doctor stated. Nor were the ulcers on Wirz's legs recent developments. They were very likely the result of scurvy, which the commandant himself had suffered while at Andersonville.

⁂

The three months of testimony finally ended on October 24, 1865. A total of 160 witnesses had been called and more than five thousand pages of testimony recorded. Within those pages were as many as four hundred objections by the counsel for defense and rulings by the court. Even before any official announcement, the *New York Times* reported that a source had told the newspaper that the court had found Wirz guilty and sentenced him to hang.

"Is it possible that I should suffer for the faults of others?" Wirz wrote in a letter to a friend who had vowed to care for his wife and his ten-year-old daughter. "There are moments when I even doubt that I was the Captain Wirz spoken of, that fiend, that devil."

The letter was never mailed. The soldier who received it for the purpose of delivery kept it as a souvenir.

The court returned its guilty verdict on both charges against Wirz, conspiracy and murder. Because the trial had been a military tribunal, however, the verdict of the court was not official until the president of the United States, Andrew Johnson, approved the decision and the sentence. There was, therefore, a final hope. Schade wrote at once to the president requesting a meeting to discuss Wirz's fate.

As the seventeenth U. S. president, successor to Abraham Lincoln, Andrew Johnson *(above)* faced many political challenges and was eventually impeached, although he was acquitted by a single vote.

"THERE ARE MOMENTS WHEN EVEN I DOUBT THAT I WAS THE CAPTAIN WIRZ SPOKEN OF, THAT FIEND, THAT DEVIL."

CHAPTER TEN
REMEMBER ANDERSONVILLE!

The testimony for the prosecution is loose, indefinite, and in the most part contradictory. Before any other court but that military commission it would have been an easy matter to uncover and bring to light . . . perjuries [false statements under oath]. . . . Time will show that this assertion of mine is no empty one.

—LOUIS SCHADE, DEFENSE ATTORNEY, OCTOBER 26, 1865

The guilty verdict had stunned Henry Wirz. He assured both of his attorneys, Louis Schade and Orrin Baker, that they had done everything possible to help him. Within days of the verdict, President Johnson had added his signature to the court's findings, making the sentence official. The president set the day of Wirz's execution for Friday, November 10, 1865.

Johnson had granted Schade a meeting, though not a private meeting, to discuss Wirz's fate. At the meeting, Schade gave the president a rather lengthy letter stating why he believed the trial had been unfair. Wirz's health was feeble, Schade told the president. His doctors believed the prisoner could not live more than six months. Let him live out his remaining days, he asked the president. He did not deserve this fate. The president promised to read Schade's letter carefully.

The construction of the scaffold in the prison yard below Wirz's room stunned the condemned man. He did not shudder at the thought of the scaffold. Rather, after months of imprisonment and of listening to lies about him in the courtroom, Wirz could not believe he would be put to death for a situation that he had found deplorable and over which he felt he had had no control.

Outside Wirz's room, a guard sat watch. Across the hallway was another prisoner—Richard Winder, the former quartermaster of Andersonville. On occasion, the guards permitted Wirz and Winder to speak to each other. At some point after his guilty verdict, Wirz had confided in Winder. His fear was that because he was so weak from illness, on the day of his execution, he might not be able to walk like a man through the prison yard to the scaffold. If he should stumble, the spectators would interpret his unsteadiness as cowardice, or worse— an indication of guilt. Wirz wanted to die like a man.

On the mantel in Wirz's room was a bottle of whiskey, perhaps given to him by his physician as a tonic for pain. He had not drunk it all.

Two days before Wirz's scheduled execution, the doors to Winder's and Wirz's cells were open. "I saw three or four men pass into his room," Winder later wrote in a letter. After the men had departed, Wirz told Winder why the men had come to see him. The men had assured him that the U.S. government would spare his life and give him his liberty if "he could give any testimony that would reflect upon Mr. [Jefferson] Davis or implicate him directly or indirectly with the condition and treatment of prisoners of war."

Wirz had been indignant. He had no personal acquaintance with the president of the Confederacy, not politically or socially. Wirz refused to save his life by becoming a traitor to the South.

⤙⟾⟾⤚

Friday morning, November 10, 1865, Wirz rose early and ate breakfast. No word had come from the president. Wirz knew that this would be his last day alive.

At eight thirty that morning, the guards allowed Richard Winder to visit with Wirz. According to news reports, the two men discussed the evidence of Wirz's trial and expressed their innocence. Winder also expressed the fear that if Wirz had been found guilty, then he would be found guilty as well when his trial came up.

When Schade arrived, a Catholic priest was in the room with Wirz. Schade told Wirz that two men had visited him last evening. They had a message from a high cabinet official, the attorney said. The president would spare his life if Wirz would implicate Jefferson Davis. The Catholic priest said he, too, had had similar visitors who had given him the same message. Wirz repeated to his attorney and to his priest what he had told the visitors who had entered his cell—he would not become a traitor to save his own life.

Schade departed some time before nine o'clock. He went directly to the White House with the intention of making a final appeal to President Johnson. Schade, at least, still had hope.

⋅⇾⇒◒⇐⇽⋅

That morning a crowd had gathered outside Old Capitol Prison. The prison yard was not very large, and only those individuals who had tickets could gain entry. More than one thousand people had applied for the two hundred admission tickets. At ten o'clock, the guards allowed the ticket holders to enter the prison yard. The hundreds of others remained in the street. Many were soldiers. Some had climbed nearby trees to see into the yard. People had gathered on the rooftops of nearby buildings. Wirz sat with his confessor, Father Boyle, and waited.

The guards came sometime after ten. They brought with them a black robe, or shroud. Wirz seemed quite calm and resigned to his fate, those who were with him would later state. He even joked about having a white robe soon. Before he left his cell, he poured some whiskey into a glass and drank it. He stroked the stray cat who had been his companion, and then he faced the guards.

They attempted to handcuff his arms behind his back, but the right arm was too swollen. Accompanied by the guards and the priest, he left his cell.

Outside, the crowd was chanting, "Remember Andersonville!" In the courtroom, Wirz had shrunk from the push of the crowd. The morning of his execution, he walked steadily and did not stumble as he had feared he might. Those who had come to see the Andersonville jailer cower and cry for mercy were disappointed. Nor was he arrogant or angry. One newspaper reporter noted Wirz had a slight smile as he climbed the scaffold.

In the courtyard was a regiment of troops in Union blue uniforms. They stood at attention, muskets shouldered. Bayonets were fixed on the end of the guns. Wirz sat on a stool while the charges against him were read aloud. Photographers aimed their cameras.

Old Capitol Prison in Washington, D.C., served as the prison for Captain Henry Wirz before and during his trial.

Captain Henry Wirz *(second from right on platform)* was the only man tried, convicted, and executed for Civil War crimes. He was hanged at One First Street Northeast in Washington, D.C., on the future site of the U.S. Supreme Court Building.

Wirz's final words were to proclaim his innocence. He shook hands with the guards. The executioner slipped a dark hood over his head and adjusted the noose around his neck. One reporter for *Frank Leslie's Illustrated Newspaper* noted that Wirz had conducted himself with dignity. Had the reporter not known the details of the trial, had he not thought of Wirz as a devil, he might have called the prisoner's behavior "heroic."

The trap was sprung, and Wirz's body fell. The rope did not immediately break his neck. When at last his struggle ended, the crowd gave a roaring cheer. The sound, said one reporter, was "just such as I have heard scores of times on the battlefield after a successful charge."

It was 10:32.

At 10:35 Schade met with President Johnson. Neither he nor the president was aware that Wirz was already dead.

And so the military tribunal had given the public Wirz. But Wirz's life was not enough to satisfy the North's desire for revenge. The press turned its attention to the next great war trial, that of the traitor Jefferson Davis.

Most Civil War historians and legal scholars would later view the Wirz trial as "a shameless charade," an effort to railroad Wirz in response to public outcry for vengeance. At the time, even Wallace's wife had begun to question whether justice was truly being served in the courtroom. The government—and her husband—seemed determined to "crush one miserable worm." Wirz was a tool, she believed—it should have been Davis and Secretary of War James Seddon who were on trial.

"If the government lets Davis go unpunished," wrote Wendell Phillips in a *New York Times* editorial, "then Wirz was murdered." Phillips was a leader in the antislavery movement prior to the war. His newspaper editorial did not state that Wirz was innocent. Rather, he charged the U.S. government with cowardice for punishing a "miserable tool" (Wirz) while allowing "the master" to escape justice.

The reading public understood Phillips's meaning that the master was the president of the Confederacy, Jefferson Davis. "Belle Isle and Libby prison were within his [Davis's] sight, and Andersonville existed by his order," Phillips stated. One year after Wirz's execution, Davis remained imprisoned at Fortress Monroe, near the capital, for treason. The U.S. government still had not brought him to trial. Because the government considered the legal issues so complex, the U.S. Supreme Court ultimately dismissed the case of *United States vs. Jefferson Davis* on February 26, 1869.

Was Wirz murdered, as Wendell Phillips suggested? Was he a tool following the orders of a master? The execution of Wirz did little to answer these questions. The controversy over the Andersonville jailer continued for decades. In 1907 the Georgia division of the Daughters of the Confederacy honored Wirz by raising money to build a memorial to him. The mission of this organization of women is to honor those Confederates who died during the war. The Wirz monument stands in the vicinity of the old stockade. The commandant died a hero, the Daughters believed. He was a martyr to the South. And yet the monument angered many others. It so angered Norton P. Chipman, for example, that he wrote a book on the Wirz trial, including hundreds of pages of testimony and justifying the court's guilty verdict. In Chipman's book, he tried and found Wirz guilty all over again.

Erected in Andersonville, Georgia, by the Daughters of the Confederacy, the purpose of the Captain Henry Wirz Memorial is stated in its inscription: "to rescue his name from the stigma attached to it by embittered prejudice."

With the passage of time, the public fever cooled. The country began to study more objectively what had happened, not only inside the stockade fence but also in the basement room of the Capitol Building, where the military tribunal had judged and sentenced Wirz. In the twenty-first century, most Civil War historians believe that the conditions inside the stockade, as well as in other Confederate prisons such as Belle Isle and Libby Prison, were not designed to torture Union soldiers. The blockade of Southern ports prevented medicines and much-needed resources from reaching the Southern states. The destruction by foraging armies had destroyed crops as well as transportation lines. A lack of effective leadership in managing the ever-growing prison populations was also a factor that led to the suffering and deaths of so many men. And yet, historians also point out that the Confederacy and its leaders knew about the devastating situation at Andersonville and allowed it to continue.

Most legal scholars also agree that the Wirz Commission was prejudiced against Wirz from the outset. Wallace had overruled many rightful objections by the counsel for the defense. The court had blocked or otherwise failed to take into account testimony that was favorable to the defendant. The tribunal found Wirz guilty of conspiracy, and yet no other conspirators were charged or tried. The tribunal found Wirz guilty of thirteen counts of murder, and yet not one of the victims had a name. Many of the witnesses who testified against Wirz had escaped from the prison. When recaptured, Wirz sentenced them to punishments in the stocks. They held grudges against him, and their perjury reflected their hatred.

The media, too, was hostile. From the onset of the war, the press had taken sides and inflamed the passions of the people on both sides. Wirz was just one of the targets of the Northern press. That he was guilty of intentionally starving and withholding medical care for prisoners, there was no doubt, stated an editorial in *Harper's Weekly* just days before the trial began. And yet Wirz was no martyr, as the Daughters of the Confederacy later claimed. He was a troubled man with an explosive temper. He verbally abused, cursed, and threatened those over whom he had authority. His prolonged illness and the impossible challenges he faced at Andersonville with little support from his Confederate superiors had overwhelmed him and ultimately destroyed him.

Those who lived through the Civil War and those who survived Andersonville and other prison pens viewed Wirz as a demon. Even after more than a century, the question remained unanswered: Was Wirz an evil man, or was it the time and place—war itself—that created the horrors of Andersonville?

EPILOGUE
AFTER ANDERSONVILLE

The great body of pen-fighters who came forward on each side as soon as the clashing of swords died away, waging a war fierce though bloodless, resembled the first troops who reached the seat of war, both in abundance of zeal and lack of knowledge. It was impossible for them to write the true history of the war.

—PROFESSOR RUFUS B. RICHARDSON, NOVEMBER 1880,
IN AN ARTICLE ABOUT THE ANDERSONVILLE PRISON CAMP

On a morning in 1902, a train pulled into Andersonville. An elderly man stepped from the train onto the platform and looked around. Not much had changed in thirty-eight years. The surrounding countryside was still green with tall pines. The same wooden building, the station depot, slumped alongside the railbed. A boy of about ten or eleven approached the man. Was he looking for a guide? He knew everything there was to tell about Andersonville, he said.

The man nodded. Yes, he would surely appreciate someone taking him around the stockade. They began the long walk through the scrub brush from the railroad to where Camp Sumter had once stood. The boy engaged the man in conversation at once, guessing from the way he talked that he was from the North. Yes, the man said, he was. James Madison Page didn't tell the boy anything else about himself. He didn't tell him that this was not the first time he had walked the grounds of the prison pen.

The stockade walls were no longer standing. Pine stumps from the palisade were all that remained. The boy led Page to the spot where a pure spring of water had bubbled from the ground. This was the

The Andersonville National Historic Site evolved through the twentieth century into the only park in the National Park System to serve as a memorial to all U.S. prisoners of war. The entryway shown here is circa 1910.

same Providence Springs that had come as the result of the terrible thunderstorm in August 1864. In the years since, citizens had erected a roof over the springs, and benches were nearby. Page sat down.

"Many years ago," the boy began to tell a story, "... there were thousands of people imprisoned, and during the late summer water became low in the creek down there and there was great suffering among the people; but there was one good man among them, and one day when the suffering was most intense this pious [religious] man knelt right down here." The boy pointed. Page looked. The man had prayed for God to send water, the boy said. "When he arose to his feet," the boy continued, "water burst out right there from under the stump and it has been flowing ever since."

Page's guide took him to other places within the stockade. Page visited that place beyond the fence where many of his friends had been buried. The cemetery was quiet, restful. Mockingbirds had returned. The air smelled sweetly of pine. The boy impressed Page with his knowledge, though the old man did not correct his errors. No one would ever know the true story of Andersonville. Even the men who had survived the pen did not agree on everything that had happened here. The only certainty was that Andersonville was a national tragedy.

On the day Wirz had died, embittered soldiers had chanted "Remember Andersonville!" The nation did. The same year the war ended, John Urban published his memoir of soldiering and of his months as an Andersonville prisoner of war. In the decades that followed, former prisoners of war published almost two hundred books on their experiences in Confederate prison camps. Among those men were John Ransom, John McElroy, Warren Lee Goss, Lessel Long, and James Madison Page. The veterans of Andersonville formed associations that met regularly. At the turn of the twentieth century, the nation began building monuments to the men who had died at Andersonville.

On May 30, 1904, the governor of Michigan traveled to Anderson Station to dedicate that state's memorial to the sons who had died inside the stockade. "Theirs was not the glory of death on the firing line," he said in his speech. "Penned in by the deadline, wasted by disease, far from home and loved ones, they were mercifully mustered out, leaving as a heritage to the nation the memory of a devotion as limitless as eternity itself."

His words were grand. So, too, were the impressive monuments that Wisconsin, Massachusetts, Illinois, Pennsylvania, Connecticut, and many other states erected. They gave glory at last to those men who believed their country had abandoned them.

The U.S. Congress stated in the authorizing legislation that Andersonville National Historic Site's purpose is "to provide an understanding of the overall prisoner-of-war story of the Civil War, to interpret the role of prisoner-of-war camps in history, to commemorate the sacrifice of Americans who lost their lives in such camps, and to preserve the monuments located within the site." Visitors can view the graves of those who died at Andersonville *(right)*, as well as the marble statue at the park's entrance *(top)*. Many state's have monuments to those who died there, such as this memorial for Michigan soldiers *(above)*.

Surviving Andersonville involved more than scrubbing lice and other vermin from the body and more than burning filthy rags and slipping into clean clothes. Survival required medical care for scurvy, dysentery, and gangrene. And once released from the hospitals, the prisoners still had to heal their minds and learn to cope with their memories.

On the pages that follow are brief descriptions of what happened to some of the major characters mentioned in this book. The names are presented alphabetically. When available, birth and death dates have been added.

DORENCE ATWATER (1845–1910) had taken his death register to Andersonville to assist Clara Barton in identifying the graves of prisoners. When he returned to Washington, D.C., the U.S. government asked him to return the rolls. The government had, in fact, copied the rolls but insisted on Atwater returning his copy as well. When he refused, the military arrested Atwater and tried him by court-martial. They charged him with theft and disobeying military orders. The court convicted Atwater, and his sentence was a dishonorable discharge, a fine of three hundred dollars, and eighteen months of hard labor. Clara Barton argued for Atwater's release, and after two months, the soldier who had risked his life to smuggle the names of almost thirteen thousand Union dead, was pardoned. Atwater would go on to live a very productive life, at one point serving as the U.S. Counsel, or representative, to the island of Tahiti in the South Pacific. He is buried in Tahiti.

ORRIN S. BAKER (ca. 1828–1889) had lived in Virginia at the start of the war but was a strong Union supporter. He moved to Washington, D.C., in 1865. A few months later, he volunteered to defend Henry Wirz. Although the press accused Baker of seeking fame by defending Wirz, Baker slipped quietly out of the spotlight after the trial ended and did not seek to capitalize on his role as the defense counsel for the Andersonville jailer. Very little is known about Baker in the later years of his life.

CLARA BARTON (1821–1912) traveled around the country, sometimes accompanied by Dorence Atwater, to speak about the Civil War and its dead and missing soldiers. She would later found the American Red Cross, an organization that assists communities during disasters.

BATTESE, a Native American soldier from Minnesota, visited John Ransom while he was recuperating from scurvy in the Marine Hospital in Savannah, Georgia. It was the last Ransom ever saw or heard from the man whom he believed saved his life. Battese likely was an alias. The author could find no mention of Battese on the records of those who were imprisoned at Andersonville.

NORTON P. CHIPMAN (1834–1924) never faltered in his belief that justice had been served by the Wirz Commission. His ambitions for a successful career were realized. He was elected to Congress as a representative of the District of Columbia in 1871. He cofounded the Grand Army of the Republic, an organization of Union veterans who had served in the Civil War. He also authored the order to create Decoration Day, a national holiday to honor veterans of the Civil War. Later, the name would be changed to Memorial Day.

JEFFERSON DAVIS (1808–1889), president of the Confederacy, was put in prison for two years after the war's end. Meanwhile, he demanded that the U.S. government place him on trial so he could prove he was innocent of treason. Not until May 1867 did the U.S. government release him on a bond of one hundred thousand dollars. Davis and his family lived in Canada for six months, returning to Richmond in the fall of 1867 for the beginning of his trial. The U.S. government, however, postponed the case. In February 1869, the government dropped all charges against Davis.

In 1890 Davis wrote and published *A Short History of the Confederate States of America* documenting the rise and fall of this Southern government. In this book, he stated with confidence that neither Wirz nor General John Winder had conspired to maliciously destroy the lives of Union prisoners under their care.

NEAL DOW (1804–1897) was exchanged on March 14, 1864. The general resigned from the military later that year. As mayor of Portland, Maine, he had devoted himself to promoting temperance. He sponsored the Maine law of 1851, which prohibited the manufacture and sale of liquor, earning himself the title Father of Prohibition.

CHARLES HOPKINS (1842–1934) left Andersonville on Sunday, September 11, 1864, certain he was bound for exchange. He was instead relocated to the prison pen at Florence, South Carolina. He was released in February 1865. He was quite ill from typhoid fever. He recovered, however, returned home, married, and fathered seven children. He remained very active as a veteran of the Civil War. He died in New Jersey.

JOHN B. JONES ended his diary on April 19, 1865. He had secured permission for himself and his wife to travel from Richmond to the eastern shore of Virginia. One of the final passages in his diary reads, "I never swore allegiance to the Confederate States, but was true to it." There is no further information on him.

ANTHONY KEILEY (1835–1905) survived his imprisonment at Elmira, New York. He returned to Virginia where he was elected mayor of Richmond in 1871. While visiting Paris, France, in 1905, his carriage collided with another, and he died from his injuries.

ROBERT KELLOGG (1844–1922) was twenty years old when he was finally exchanged in November 1864. He returned to his hometown in

Connecticut for rest and recuperation but returned to military service at Annapolis, Maryland. His duty was to assist in processing thousands of returning prisoners, many of whom had suffered as much as he. In 1865 he published his memoir, *Life and Death in Rebel Prisons.*

In the Andersonville prison pen, a common experience was to wake in the morning and discover two or three comrades lying nearby who had died in the night. "A prisoner is condemned to these things," wrote Robert Kellogg a few months after he regained his freedom and had returned to Connecticut. "He must steel himself against that which once would have sent sympathy through his whole being—a gushing tide."

LEROY KEY (ca. 1840–1880) was assigned for work in the Andersonville bakehouse outside the stockade after the hanging of the five Raiders. In September 1864, he appealed to Wirz to be exchanged with those prisoners being released. When Wirz refused, Key escaped but was later recaptured. He fell ill and was eventually released with sick prisoners before the end of 1864. He never completely regained robust health, for which he had been known before his capture. When he died in Chicago, Illinois, the *New York Times* ran an obituary, describing Key as a natural leader and a man of strong constitution whose imprisonment at Andersonville had likely contributed to his early death.

LESSEL LONG (1838–1915) also survived his imprisonment at Andersonville and returned home. After twenty years, however, Long still woke from his sleep with the groans of starving men in his ears. Talking about the experience could sometimes help relieve his painful memories, but the details were too grim. People often thought that perhaps the Andersonville survivors were exaggerating the suffering, but only the "grizzled veteran" can realize the horror of a year's imprisonment in the rebel camps, Long later wrote in his memoir of the war, *Twelve Months in Andersonville*.

JOHN MCELROY (1846–1929) survived Andersonville and returned to Ohio, where he married and became a writer for various newspapers and magazines. He first began writing about his Andersonville experience on the encouragement of one of his editors. His columns appeared in Ohio newspapers and generated thousands of letters from appreciative readers. He would go on to write a lengthy nonfiction book on the prison pen titled *This Was Andersonville*, which is still available in libraries and online. In 1884 McElroy moved from Ohio to Washington, D.C., to become the editor and co-owner of the *National Tribune* newspaper.

JOHN RANSOM (1843–1919) prided himself on not crying when he saw the suffering and cruelty around him at Andersonville. The train

that carried him away from Andersonville stopped at Savannah, Georgia. There, laid alongside the railroad bed, he waited while the others who could still walk went to a new prison. The guards carried Ransom to a hospital. While he began to regain his health and his strength, he would often break down and cry.

In the hospital, Ransom was still a prisoner of the Confederacy. His nurses burned his ragged clothing and washed him and then washed him again, slowly peeling away the layers of pine soot. The bed, too, was clean. His meals were gruel at first, for that was all his shrunken stomach could hold. But it was nourishing. While a prisoner at Belle Isle and then at Andersonville, Ransom had lost a great deal of weight. Those in the hospital guessed Ransom weighed only about 95 pounds (43 kg). As weeks passed, the swelling in his legs went down. His appetite returned. He was often irritable. Those were signs that he would survive after all, the doctors said. By October 1864, Ransom's eyesight had improved so that he could once again read and write in his diary.

Once Ransom regained his health enough to travel, the guards marched him to the trains and another ride in a boxcar to another prison camp. This time, Ransom had the strength and determination to jump from the car. He escaped with a few others, and soon they were once again behind Union lines. Ransom returned to his home in Jackson, Michigan, and married. He later moved to Chicago. He published his diary in 1881, hoping in part to earn a little cash from it. His memoir, *John Ransom's Andersonville Diary*, continues to inform readers about the ghastly horrors of war imprisonment and is available both in print through bookstores and online in digital format.

PRESCOTT TRACY was called to Washington, D.C., to give testimony against Henry Wirz. Tracy reportedly had referred to him as a brute and a monster during his imprisonment at Andersonville. Tracy did not see Wirz commit acts of cruelty on prisoners, he testified, but he heard the commandant give orders to the guards to shoot anyone who crossed into the deadline. Nothing more is known of Tracy.

JOHN W. URBAN (1844–1918), also known at Andersonville as John Dowd, was exchanged in December 1864. Soon after boarding the *New York*, a Union ship, he removed his clothing and dropped them and his blanket into the sea. Without regret, he watched his clothes and his lice float away. After a warm bath, he received a clean "suit of Uncle Sam's blue." He arrived by ship at Annapolis, Maryland, on December 19. Family and friends crowded the wharves and shoreline, looking anxiously for the face of a son, a father, a brother, or a friend. Urban remembered that a band played "Home, Sweet Home." Like so many released prisoners, Urban was hospitalized. His medical care continued for seven months, and though he survived, he never returned to good health. In 1886 he published his memoir *Battlefield and Prison Pen*.

LEW WALLACE (1827–1905) became a best-selling author. In 1880 the major general wrote a historical novel about ancient Rome titled *Ben-Hur*. The book became a nineteenth-century best-seller and remains in print. Wallace's book was made into four different movies. The most famous movie version, made in 1959, starred Charlton Heston as Ben-Hur.

RICHARD WINDER remained in Old Capitol Prison until December 1865. Then the U.S. government sent the captain to Richmond, Virginia, to be tried for treason. Months passed, however, without the government moving forward on the trial. Eventually, Winder was released from prison, apparently because the U.S. government felt it did not have enough evidence to find him guilty.

SOURCE NOTES

14 *Richmond Daily Dispatch*, "The Yankee Prisoners and Commissary Northrop," December 27, 1863, Civil War Richmond, n.d., http://imls.richmond .edu/cgi/t/text/text-idx?c=ddr;cc=ddr;q1= december%2022%2C%201863;rgn=div3;view=text; idno=ddr0973.0025.145;node=ddr0973.0025.145% 3A8.1.1 (January 21, 2009).

15 John Ransom, *Andersonville Diary, Escape and List of the Dead with Name, Co., Regiment, Date of Death and No. of Grave in Cemetery* (Philadel-phia: Douglass Bros., 1883), 16.

15 Ibid., 19.

18 William Best Hesseltine, ed., *Civil War Prisons* (Kent, OH: Kent State University Press, 1962), 68.

19 U.S. War Department, *The War of Rebellion: A Compilation of the Official Records of the Union and Confederate Armies*, ser. 2 (Washington, DC: Government Printing Office, 1880–1901), 6: 612.

19 J. B. Jones, *A Rebel War Clerk's Diary*, November 13, 1863, 96, available online at Perseus Digital Library, n.d., http://www.perseus.tufts.edu/ hopper/text.jsp?doc=Perseus%3Atext%3A2001.05 .0022%3Achapter%3D33 (January 21, 2009).

23 *New York Herald*, "Our Captured Correspondent," May 9, 1863, Civil War Richmond, January 10, 2009, http://www.mdgorman.com/Prisons/our_ captured_correspondent.htm (January 21, 2009).

24 Hesseltine, 64.

24 Ransom, 26.

25 James Madison Page, *The True Story of Andersonville Prison: A Defense of Major Henry Wirz* (New York: Neale Publishing Co., 1908), 52.

26 *Richmond Sentinel*, "Change of Base," December 30, 1863, Civil War Richmond, January 10, 2009, http://www.mdgorman.com/Written_Accounts/ Sentinel/1863/richmond_sentinel,_12_30_1863 .htm (January 21, 2009).

30 *New York Times*, "Where Our Prisoners Are Go-ing," March 13, 1864, 4, n.d., http://query.nytimes .com/gst/abstract.html?res=990DE6D6173EEE34 BC4B52DFB566838F679FDE&scp=1&sq=%22 Where+our+prisoners+are+going%22&st=p (January 27, 2009).

31 Jones, February 17, 1864, 152, available online at Perseus Digital Library, January 10, 2009, http://

www.perseus.tufts.edu/hopper/text.jsp?doc= Perseus%3Atext%3A2001.05.0022%3Achapter% 3D36 (January 27, 2009).

32 U.S. War Department, ser. 2, 6: 914, 985.

35 "When Johnny Comes Marching Home," Philadelphia: Johnson & Co., n.d., as reprinted on "America Singing: Nineteenth-Century Song Sheets," American Memory, Library of Congress, n.d., http://lcweb2.loc.gov/diglib/ihas/loc.rbc .cw.106520/default.html (January 26, 2009).

35 William B. Styple and John J. Fitzpatrick, eds., *The Andersonville Diary of Charles Hopkins, 1st New Jersey Infantry* (Kearny, NJ: Belle Grove Publishing Co., 1988), 62.

37 Richard W. Lobst, *Civil War Macon* (Macon, GA: Mercer University Press, 1999), 126.

38 T. H. Mann, "A Yankee in Andersonville," *Century Magazine* 40, no. 1 (July 1890): 453.

39 John McElroy, *This Was Andersonville; The True Story of Andersonville Military Prison as Told in the Personal Recollections of John McElroy, Sometime Private, Co. L, 16th Illinois Cavalry*, ed. Roy Meredith (New York: Fairfax Press, 1957), 7.

39 Ransom, 55.

40 Philip Burnham, *So Far from Dixie: Confederates in Yankee Prisons* (Lanham, MD: Taylor Trade Publishers, 2003), 39.

42 Edward D. Jevey and Henry S. White, eds., *Prison Life among the Rebels: Recollections of a Union Chaplain* (Kent, OH: Kent State University Press, 1990), 37.

44 Page, 91.

47–48 Ransom, 58.

48–49 McElroy, 19.

51 Ovid L. Futch., *History of Andersonville Prison* (Gainesville: University of Florida Press, 1968), 34.

51 U.S. War Department, ser. 2, 7: 207.

53 Ransom, 65.

54 Mann, 453.

54 Ibid., 454.

54–55 Warren Lee Goss, *The Soldier's Story of His Captivity at Andersonville, Belle Isle, and Other Rebel Prisons* (Boston: Lee & Shepard, 1866), 71.

56 Ransom, 70.

56 U.S. War Department, ser. 2, 7: 169–170.

56 Ibid., 170.

56 Ibid., 136.

57 Ibid., 167–168.

58–59 U.S. War Department, ser. 2, 7: 403.

60 Robert Kellogg, *Life and Death in Rebel Prisons* (Hartford, CT: L. Stebbins, 1865), 109–110, available online at Google Books, 2009, http://books .google.com/books?id=ywsTAAAAYAAJ (October 7, 2009).

66 N. P. Chipman, *The Tragedy of Andersonville: The Trial of Henry Wirz, the Prison Keeper* (Sacramento, CA: privately printed, 1911), 91, 186.

66 McElroy, 166.

71 Orson Blair, *History of the Twenty-Fourth Michigan of the Iron Brigade* (Detroit: Winn & Hammond, 1891), 451.

72 U.S. War Department, ser. 2, 7: 522.

72 Mann, 450.

73 U.S. War Department, ser. 2, 7: 522.

73 Styple and Fitzpatrick, 117–123.

74 W. L. Kingsley, "Andersonville," *New England and Yale Review* 39, no. 157 (September 1880): 757.

74 Kellogg, 107–109.

75 Library of Congress, *Trial of Henry Wirz.* House Executive document 23, 40th Congress, 2nd session (Washington, DC: Government Printing Office, 1868), 712.

76 Page, 97.

77 Ibid.

78 Cornelius Van Santvoord, *The One Hundred and Twentieth Regiment New York State Volunteers: A Narrative of Its Services in the War for the Union* (Roundout, NY: Press of the Kingston Freeman, 1894), 10.

80 David Kennedy, diary excerpt, available online at "Social Aspects of the Civil War," *National Park Service,* n.d., http://www.itd.nps.gov/cwss/ manassas/social/andersonville.htm (January 21, 2009).

80 Styple and Fitzpatrick, 86–87.

81 John Howard Stibbs, "Andersonville and the Trial of Henry Wirz," *Iowa Journal of History* 9 (January 1911): 47.

82 U.S. War Department, ser. 2, 7: 522, 708.

84 John Urban, *Battlefield and Prison Pen: Or Through the War and Thrice a Prisoner in Rebel Dungeons* (Philadelphia: Edgewood Publishing Co., 1882), 307.

85 Ibid., 318.

86 Robert S. Davis, *Ghosts and Shadows of Andersonville: Essays on the Secret Social Histories of America's Deadliest Prison* (Macon, GA: Mercer University Press, 2006), 240. Originally published in the *New York Mercury,* August 20, 1865, from file Apz (EB) 1865, Entry 409, Records of the Adjutant General, Record Group 94, National Archives and Records Administration.

87 Ibid., 238.

89 Ransom, 108.

89 Ibid., 108.

91 Davis, 238–239.

92 Ibid., 245.

93–94 Library of Congress, *Trial,* 428.

94 Page, 116.

95 Urban, 332.

95 Futch, 73.

95 William Marvel, *Andersonville: The Last Depot* (Chapel Hill: University of North Carolina Press, 1994), 143.

96 Urban, 335.

96 Ransom, 117.

96 Urban, 324–325.

97 McElroy, 65, 127, 146.

98 U.S. War Department, ser. 2, 7: 607.

99 Bruce Catton, *The American Heritage New History of the Civil War* (New York: Viking, 1996), 379.

99 Ibid.

101 Library of Congress, *Trial,* 187–188.

101 Ibid., 280.

101 Ibid., 326.

103 U.S. War Department, ser. 2, 7: 619.

104 *Harper's Weekly,* "Rebel Cruelty," June 18, 1864, 387, available online at the Civil War Website, n.d., http://www.sonofthesouth.net/leefoundation/ civil-war/1864/june/cold-harbor-battle.htm (January 26, 2009).

105 Walter Clark, ed., *Histories of the Several Regiments and Battalions from North Carolina, in the Great War 1861–'65* (Goldsboro, NC: Nash Brothers Book and Job Printers, 1901), 681–682.

105 Lonnie R. Speer, *War of Vengeance: Acts of Retaliation against Civil War POWs* (Mechanicsburg, PA: Stackpole Books, 2002), 87.

106 U.S. War Department, ser. 2, 7: 622.

107 Ibid., 170–171, 426–427, 524–525; Library of Congress, *Trial*, 230.

107 Ibid., 759.

108 Rufus B. Richardson, "Andersonville," *New Englander and Yale Review* 39, no.157 (September 1880), 1,880, 729–744.

108 Doris Kearns Goodwin, *Team of Rivals: The Political Genius of Abraham Lincoln* (New York: Simon & Schuster, 2006), 645.

108 *New York Times*, "The Union Prisoners at Andersonville," August 24, 1864, 4, n.d., http://query.nytimes.com/gst/abstract.ht (January 27, 2009).

109 U.S. War Department, ser. 2, 7: 767–768.

110 Ibid., 294.

111 Ibid.

112 Ransom, 133.

113 U.S. War Department, ser. 2, 7: 589.

118 Kellogg, 283.

119 Page, 164.

120 Speer, 87.

121 *New York Times*, "A Grand Victory for Humanity," October 28, 1864, 4, n.d., http://query.nytimes.com/gst/abstract.html?res=9907E6DC153EEE34BC4051DFB667838F679FDE&scp=19&sq=andersonville&st=p (January 2, 2009).

122 *New York Times*, "Our Prisoners, Their Release from Captivity," November 24, 1864, 1, n.d., http://query.nytimes.com/gst/abstract.html?res=9F01E0DB153EEE34BC4E51DFB767838F679FDE&scp=26&sq=andersonville&st=p (January 21, 2009).

123–124 Richard Taylor, *Destruction and Reconstruction: Personal Experiences of the Late War* (New York: D. Appleton and Co., 1879), 216.

125 U.S. War Department, ser. 1, part 2, 49: 800.

126 Ibid., ser. 2, 8: 735.

126–127 Jones, 465.

127 Ibid., 471.

130 Library of Congress, *Trial*, 20.

130 U.S. War Department, ser. 2, 8: 537–538.

131 Ibid., 558.

132 Library of Congress, *Trial*, 20.

133 Chipman, 27.

137 Ibid., 320.

137 Charles Sumner Young, *Clara Barton: A Centenary Tribute to the World's Greatest Humanitarian* (Boston: R. G. Badger, 1922), 332, available online at Google Books, n.d., http://books.google.com/books?id=52kDAAAAYAAJ&printsec=frontcover&dq=clara+barton&as_brr=1#PPA337,M1 (January 27, 2009).

138 Chipman, 483.

138 Young, 332.

140 Library of Congress, "Andersonville," American Treasures of the Library of Congress, June 24, 2005, http://www.loc.gov/exhibits/treasures/trm111.html (January 21, 2009).

141 *New York Times*, "An Incarnate Fiend," August 3, 1865, 1, n.d., http://query.nytimes.com/gst/abstract.html?res=9C03E2D8123EEE34BC4C53DFBE66838E679FDE&scp=3&sq=wertz&st=p (January 21, 2009).

141 *New York Times*, "More Evidence of Rebel Brutality," August 8,1864, n.d., http://query.nytimes.com/gst/abstract.html?res=9A07E6D81330EF34BC4053DFBE66838E679FDE&scp=4&sq=wertz&st=p (January 21, 2009).

141 *New York Times*, "The Keeper of the Andersonville Prison—Confession and Avoidance," August 4, 1864, 4, n.d., http://query.nytimes.com/gst/abstract.html?res=9F05E1D8123EEE34BC4C53DFBE66838E679FDE&scp=2&sq=wertz&st=p (January 21, 2009).

142 Young, 337.

143 Ibid., 336.

144 *New York Times*, "Wirz and the Union Prisoners," August 31, 1865, 4, n.d., http://query.nytimes.com/gst/abstract.html?res=9901E0D6123EEE34BC4950DFBE66838E679FDE&scp=17&sq=wirz&st=p (January 21, 2009).

144 Lewis L. Laska and James Smith, "Hell and the Devil: Andersonville and the Trial of Captain Henry Wirz, C. S. A., 1865," *Military Law Review* 68 (Spring 1977): 78.

145 Lew Wallace, *An Autobiography*, Vol. 2. (New York: Harper & Brothers Pub., 1906), 854.

145 Ibid.

145 Library of Congress, *Trial*, 3.

146 *New York Times*, "The Prisoner Wirz," August 23, 1865, 1, n.d., http://query.nytimes.com/gst/abstract.html?res=9B03E6D6123EEE34BC4B51DFBE66838E679FDE&scp=3&sq=wirz&st=p (January 21, 2009).

146–147 *New York Times*, "Pen Pictures of Prisoner, Counsel and Court," August 23, 1863, 1, n.d., http://query.nytimes.com/gst/abstract.html?res=990CE5DC1E3DE53BBC4D51DFBE66838E679FDE&scp=8&sq=WIRZ&st=p (January 21, 20009).

147 Library of Congress, *Trial*, 456.

147 Ibid., 463.

147 Ibid.

148 Ibid., 31.

149 Ibid., 62–63.

150 Michael Golay, *A Ruined Land: The End of the Civil War* (New York: Wiley, 1999), 276–277.

151 Library of Congress, *Trial*, 62–63.

151 Ibid., 171.

151 Ibid., 282.

151–152 Ibid.

153 Ibid., 290.

153–154 Ibid., 426.

154 Ibid., 429.

155 Page, 207.

156 Chipman, 287–288.

156 Ibid., 299.

156 Library of Congress, *Trial*, 689.

157 Ibid., 150.

158 Library of Congress, *Trial*, 803.

159 Golay, 281.

160 U.S. War Department, ser. 2, 8: 773–774.

161 Davis, 499.

163 *New York Times*, "The Final Intercession," November 11, 1864, 1, n.d., http://query.nytimes.com/gst/abstract.html?res=9503EFDF143CE63ABC4952DFB767838E679FDE&scp=3&sq=wirz+schade&st=plll (January 29, 2009).

164 Laska and Smith, 129.

164 *New York Times*, "Execution of Wirz," November 1, 1864, 1, n.d., http://query.nytimes.com/gst/abstract.html?res=9403EFDF143CE63ABC4952DFB767838E679FDE&scp=1&sq=%93Execution+of+Wirz%2C%94+&st=p (January 21, 2009).

165 Golay, 280.

165 *New York Times*, "Jefferson Davis' Release," May 30, 1867, 1, n.d., http://query.nytimes.com/gst/abstract.html?res=9B00E7D6133AEF34BC4850DFB366838C679FDE&scp=1&sq=%22Jefferson+davis+release%22&st=p (January 21, 2009).

168 Richardson, 729.

169 Page, 141–142.

169 Jones, 479.

170 "Speech of Acceptance, Gov. A. T. Bliss," *Report of the Michigan Andersonville Monument on Erection of Monument at Andersonville, Georgia* (Lansing, MI: Robert Smith Printing Co., 1905), 15.

175 Kellogg, 39.

176 Lessel Long, *Twelve Months in Andersonville: On the March—In the Battle—In the Rebel Prison Pens, and At Last in God's Country* (Huntington, IN: Thad and Mark Butler Publishers, 1886), 6.

176 Urban, 476, 478.

SELECTED BIBLIOGRAPHY

Barton, William Eleazar. *The Life of Clara Barton: Founder of the American Red Cross*. New York: Houghton Mifflin, 1922.

Benedict, George Grenville. *Vermont in the Civil War*. Burlington, VT: Free Press Association, 1888.

Blair, Orson. *History of the Twenty-Fourth Michigan of the Iron Brigade*. Detroit: Winn & Hammond, 1891.

Blaisdell, Bob. *The Civil War: A Book of Quotations*. Mineola, NY: Courier Dover Publications, 2004.

Buchanan, Lamont. *A Pictorial History of the Confederacy*. New York: Crown Pub., 1951.

Burnham, Philip. *So Far from Dixie: Confederates in Yankee Prisons*. Lanham, MD: Taylor Trade Publishing, 2003.

Catton, Bruce. *The American Heritage New History of the Civil War*. New York: Viking, 1996.

Chesnut, Mary. *A Diary from Dixie*. Rev. ed. 1905. Reprint, New York: Barnes & Noble, 2006.

Chipman, N. P. *The Tragedy of Andersonville: The Trial of Henry Wirz, the Prison Keeper*. Sacramento, CA: privately printed, 1911.

Cimbala, Paul A., and Randall M. Miller, eds. *Union Soldiers and the Northern Home Front: Wartime Experiences, Postwar Adjustments*. New York: Fordham U.P., 2002.

Clark, Walter, ed. *Histories of the Several Regiments and Battalions from North Carolina, in the Great War 1861–'65*. Goldsboro, NC: Nash Brothers, Book and Job Printers, 1901.

Cunningham, H. H. *Doctors in Gray*. Baton Rouge: Louisiana State University Press, 1958.

Davidson, Henry M. *Fourteen Months in Southern Prisons; Being a Narrative of the Treatment of Federal Prisoners of War in the Rebel Military Prisons of Richmond, Danville, Andersonville, Savannah and Millen*. Milwaukee: Daily Wisconsin Printing House, 1865.

Davis, Jefferson. *The Rise and Fall of the Confederate Government*. New York: D. Appleton & Co., 1881. Available online at Google Books. 2009. http://books.google.com/books?id=BQ4TAAAAYAAJ (January 26, 2009).

Davis, Robert S. *Ghosts and Shadows of Andersonville: Essays on the Secret Social Histories of America's Deadliest Prison*. Macon, GA: Mercer University Press, 2006.

Davis, Robert Scott, "Near Andersonville: An Historical Note on Civil War Legend and Reality. *Journal of African American History* 92, no. 1 (Winter 2007): 96.

Day, John. *The History of the Nineteenth Regiment of Maine Volunteer Infantry, 1862–1865*. Minneapolis: Great Western Printing Co., 1908. Available online at Google Books. 2009. http://books.google.com/books?id=fRRCAAAAIAAJ (January 26, 2009).

Dickey, Luther. *History of the 103rd Regiment Pennsylvania Veteran Volunteer Infantry, 1861–1865*. Chicago: Luther Dickey, 1910.

Futch, Ovid L. *History of Andersonville Prison*. Gainesville: University of Florida Press, 1968.

Golay, Michael. *A Ruined Land: The End of the Civil War*. New York: Wiley, 1999.

Goodwin, Doris Kearns. *Team of Rivals: The Political Genius of Abraham Lincoln*. New York: Simon & Schuster, 2006.

Goss, Warren Lee. *The Soldier's Story of His Captivity at Andersonville, Belle Isle, and Other Rebel Prisons*. Boston: Lee & Shepard, 1866. Available online at Google Books. 2009. http://books.google.com/books?id=WUpIdi9GIX8C (January 26, 2009).

Gresham, John M. *Historical and Biographical Record of Douglas County, Illinois*. Loganport, IN: Wilson, Humphreys & Co., 1900.

Harper's Weekly. "Rebel Cruelty." June 18, 1864, 387. Available online at the Civil War Website. N.d. http://www.sonofthesouth.net/leefoundation/civil-war/1864/june/cold-harbor-battle.htm (January 26, 2009).

Harrold, John. *The Imprisonment, Escape and Rescue of John H. Harrold, A Union Soldier in the War of the Rebellion*. Philadelphia: B. Selheimer, 1870.

Hesseltine, William Best, ed. *Civil War Prisons*. Kent, OH: Kent State University Press, 1962.

Hopkins, Charles. *The Andersonville Diary & Memoirs of Charles Hopkins, 1st New Jersey Infantry*. Edited by William B. Styple and John J. Fitzpatrick. Kearny, NJ: Belle Grove Publishing, 1988.

Horigan, Michael. *Elmira: Death Camp of the North*. Mechanicsburg, PA: Stackpole Books, 2002.

Jevey, Edward D., and Henry S. White, eds. *Prison Life among the Rebels: Recollections of a Union Chaplain*. Kent, OH: Kent State University Press, 1990.

Jones, J. B. *A Rebel War Clerk's Diary*. Available online at Perseus Digital Library. N.d. http://www.perseus.tufts.edu/hopper/text.jsp?doc=Perseus%3Atext%3A2001.05.0022%3Achapter%3D33 (January 21, 2009).

Kellogg, Robert. *Life and Death in Rebel Prisons*. Hartford, CT: L. Stebbins, 1865. Available online at Google Books. 2009. http://books.google.com/books?id=ywsTAAAAYAAJ (October 7, 2009).

Kingsley, W. L. "Andersonville." *New England and Yale Review* 39, no.157 (September 1880): 757.

Kunhardt, Philip B., Jr., and Peter W. Kunhardt. *Lincoln, An Illustrated Biography*. New York: Alfred A. Knopf, 1992.

Laska, Lewis L., and James Smith. "Hell and the Devil: Andersonville and the Trial of Captain Henry Wirz, C. S. A., 1865." *Military Law Review* 68 (Spring 1977): 77–133.

Lobst, Richard W. *Civil War Macon*. Macon, GA: Mercer University Press, 1999.

Long, Lessel. *Twelve Months in Andersonville: On the March—In the Battle—In the Rebel Prison Pens, and At Last in God's Country*. Huntington, IN: Thad and Mark Butler Publishers, 1886.

Mann, T. H., "A Yankee in Andersonville." *Century Magazine* 40, no. 1 (July 1890), 447–460, 606–623.

Marvel, William. *Andersonville: The Last Depot*. Chapel Hill: University of North Carolina Press, 1994.

McElroy, John. *This Was Andersonville; The True Story of Andersonville Military Prison as Told in the Personal Recollections of John McElroy, Sometime Private, Co. L, 16th Illinois Cavalry*. Edited by Roy Meredith. New York: Fairfax Press, 1957.

McPhearson, James. *The American Heritage New History of the Civil War*. New York: Oxford University Press, 1988.

New York Times. "How Secession Is Regarded." December 12, 1860, 1. N.d. http://query.nytimes.com/gst/abstract.html?res=9C00EEDC133DE73ABC4A51DFB467838B679FDE&scp=2&sq=secession&st=p (January 26, 2009).

Page, James Madison. *The True Story of Andersonville Prison: A Defense of Major Henry Wirz*. New York: Neale Publishing Co., 1908.

Ransom, John. *Andersonville Diary, Escape and List of the Dead with Name, Co., Regiment, Date of Death and No. of Grave in Cemetery.* Philadelphia: Douglass Bros., 1883. Available online at Google Books. 2009. http://books.google.com/books?id=iLtPHk0Yt30C (January 21, 2009).

Richardson, Rufus B. "Andersonville." *New Englander and Yale Review* 39, no. 157 (September 1880), 729–774.

Richmond Sentinel. "Yankee Prisoners." October 23, 1863. Available online at Civil War Richmond. January 9, 2009. http://mdgorman.com/Written_Accounts/Sentinel/1863/richmond_sentinel_10231863b .htm (January 26, 2009).

Sanders, Charles W., Jr. *While in the Hands of the Enemy: Military Prisons of the Civil War.* Baton Rouge: Louisiana State University Press, 2005.

Speer, Lonnie R. *War of Vengeance: Acts of Retaliation Against Civil War POWs.* Mechanicsburg, PA: Stackpole Books, 2002.

Stibbs, John Howard. "Andersonville and the Trial of Henry Wirz." *Iowa Journal of History* 9 (January 1911): 33–56.

Styple, William B., and John J. Fitzpatrick, eds. *The Andersonville Diary of Charles Hopkins, 1st New Jersey Infantry.* Kearny, NJ: Belle Grove Publishing Co., 1988.

Taylor, Richard. *Destruction and Reconstruction: Personal Experiences of the Late War.* New York: D. Appleton and Co., 1879.

Urban, John. *Battlefield and Prison Pen: Or Through the War and Thrice a Prisoner in Rebel Dungeons.* Philadelphia: Edgewood Publishing Co., 1882.

U.S. Sanitary Commission. *Narrative of Privations and Sufferings of United States Officers and Soldiers While Prisoners of War in the Hands of the Rebel Authorities: Being a Report of a Commission of Inquiry.* Philadelphia: King & Baird, 1864.

U.S. War Department. *Trial of Henry Wirz.* House Executive document 23. 40th Congress, 2nd session. Washington, DC: Government Printing Office, 1868.

———. *The War of Rebellion: A Compilation of the Official Records of the Union and Confederate Armies.* Ser. 2. Vols. 6–8. Washington, DC: Government Printing Office, 1880–1901.

Van Santvoord, Cornelius. *The One Hundred and Twentieth Regiment New York State Volunteers: A Narrative of Its Services in the War for the Union.* Roundout, NY: Press of the Kingston Freeman, 1894.

Wallace, Lew. *An Autobiography.* Vol. 2. New York: Harper & Brothers Pub., 1906.

Weber, Mark. "Civil War Concentration Camps," *Journal for Historical Review* 2, no. 2 (Summer 1981): 137.

Young, Charles Sumner. *Clara Barton: A Centenary Tribute to the World's Greatest Humanitarian.* Boston: R. G. Badger, 1922. Available online at Google Books. N.d. http://books.google.com/books?id=52kDA AAAYAAJ&printsec=frontcover&dq=clara+barton&as_brr=1#PPA337,M1 (January 27, 2009).

FURTHER READING, FILM, AND WEBSITES

BOOKS

Arnold, James R. *The Civil War.* Minneapolis: Lerner Publications Company, 2005.

Arnold, James R., and Roberta Wiener. *Divided in Two: The Road to Civil War, 1861.* Minneapolis: Twenty-First Century Books, 2002.

———. *Life Goes On: The Civil War at Home, 1861–1865.* Minneapolis: Twenty-First Century Books, 2002.

———. *Lost Cause: The End of the Civil War, 1864–1865.* Minneapolis: Twenty-First Century Books, 2002.

———. *On to Richmond: The Civil War in the East, 1861–1862.* Minneapolis: Twenty-First Century Books, 2002.

———. *River to Victory: The Civil War in the West, 1861–1863.* Minneapolis: Twenty-First Century Books, 2002.

———. *This Unhappy Country: The Turn of the Civil War, 1863.* Minneapolis: Twenty-First Century Books, 2002.

Burnham, Philip. *So Far from Dixie: Confederates in Yankee Prisons.* New York: Taylor Trade Publishing, 2003.

Damon, Duane. *Growing Up in the Civil War 1861 to 1865.* Minneapolis: Lerner Publications Company, 2003.

Day, Nancy. *Your Travel Guide to Civil War America.* Minneapolis: Twenty-First Century Books, 2001.

Donahue, John. *An Island Far from Home.* Minneapolis: Carolrhoda Books, 1995.

Hackman, Gene, and Daniel Lenihan. *Escape from Andersonville: A Novel of the Civil War.* New York: Macmillan, 2008.

Kantor, MacKinlay. *Andersonville.* New York: Plume, 1993.

Pucci, Kelly. *Camp Douglas: Chicago's Civil War Prison.* Chicago: Arcadia Publishing, 2007.

FILM

"Andersonville." DVD. Directed by John Frankenheimer. Atlanta: Turner Television Network. 1989. This made-for-television miniseries was nominated for seven Emmys and won an Emmy for Outstanding Individual Achievement in Directing for a Miniseries or a Special.

WEBSITES

Andersonville

> http://www.nps.gov/ande/index.htm
> This site, maintained by the U.S. National Park Service, provides an overview of the prisoner-of-war camp along with interesting photographs and trivia information. The camp became a national cemetery in July 1865, soon after the last prisoners were released. The U.S. Army maintained the property for many years. In 1970 the land became an official national park. The site is also home to the National Prisoner of War Museum. This museum's collection explores the experiences of all prisoners of war and not just those held captive during the U.S. Civil War.

Andersonville National Historic Site

> http://www.npca.org/stateoftheparks/andersonville
> The National Park Conservation Association (NPCA) provides a downloadable Adobe publication on the history of Andersonville. Included are fascinating contemporary photographs of the national park, including memorials and sculptures.

The Civil War

> http://www.sonofthesouth.net/leefoundation/the-civil-war.htm
> More than seven thousand pages of original Civil War content have been digitized on this site, including postings of *Harper's Weekly* magazine. This site provides original illustrations, eye-witness accounts of battles, and commentary on events and key military leaders.

Civil War Richmond

> http://mdgorman.com
> This research site includes Civil War-era documents, photographs, and maps relating to Richmond, Virginia, the capital of the Confederacy. News articles as well as reports cover a diversity of topics, from food shortages to prisoner-of-war camps and Confederate hospitals.

Index of Civil War Information Available on the Net

> http://www.civilwarhome.com/indexcivilwarinfo.htm
> This is a link index that provides hot links to Civil War websites that provide information on a wide range of topics, including everything from Civil War clothing to weapons and battles. Initially published by Louisiana State University's Civil War Center, the compilation of links is impressive.

The Trial of Captain Henry Wirz

> http://www.law.umkc.edu/faculty/projects/ftrials/Wirz/Wirz.htm
> The Missouri-Kansas City School of Law published this site as part of its Famous Trials Seminar. The materials presented here include excerpts from the trial, biographies of key figures associated with both the prosecution and the defense of Henry Wirz, plus a discussion of the trial's legal controversies. Also included is a death log from Andersonville, based on Dorence Atwater's records, providing the total number of deaths each day of each month during the period in which the prisoner-of-war camp was operational.

The Valley of the Shadow

> http://valley.vcdh.virginia.edu/
> This site explores life during the U.S. Civil War as seen through the eyes of two communities, the Northern region of Franklin County, Pennsylvania, and the Southern region of Augusta County, Virginia. Letters, diaries, newspaper articles, maps, and even church records reveal the fears and hopes of the ordinary people who lived in these towns during the war years.

INDEX

PHOTO ACKNOWLEDGMENTS

The images in this book are used with the permission of: Library of Congress, pp. 3 (LC-USZ62-82976), 17 (LC-USZ62-25518), 19 (LC-DIG-cwpb-04402), 21 (LC-DIG-cwpb-00768), 22 (LC-DIG-cwpb-03819), 25 (left, LC-DIG-ppmsca-19305), 25 (right, LC-DIG-cwpbh-00958), 27 (bottom, LC-USZ62-57508), 31 (LC-USZ62-20961), 33 (LC-DIG-cwpb-02734), 38–39 (LC-USZ62-149), 45 (LC-USZ6-10002), 46 (LC-USZ62-34419), 53 (LC-USZ62-15653), 55 (LC-USZ62-198), 57 (LC-DIG-ppmsca-10762), 60–61 (LC-DIG-pga-02585), 65 (LC-USZ62-82976), 68 (LOT 7361), 77 (LC-DIG-pga-01846), 82, 88 (LC-USZ62-34422), 90 (LC-DIG-cwpbh-03240), 94 (LC-USZ62-34420), 109 (LC-DIG-ppmsca-05574), 112 (LC-USZC4-10808), 114–115 (LC-USZ62-34423), 117 (LC-USZ62-40095), 123 (LC-DIG-cwpb-06291), 127 (LC-DIG-ppmsca-08230), 129 (LC-DIG-npcc-19653), 133 (LC-DIG-cwpbh-00110), 134 (LC-USZ62-62748), 140 (LC-DIG-ppmsca-05602), 142 (LC-USZ62-93979), 150 (LC-DIG-cwpbh-00933), 159 (LC-USZ62-13017), 163 (LC-DIG-ppmsca-12611), 164 (LC-DIG-cwpb-04194), 172 (LC-USZ62-62748), 174 (top, LC-DIG-cwpbh-00110), 179 (top, LC-DIG-cwpbh-00933); The Granger Collection, New York, p. 8; © iStockphoto .com/Daniel Cooper, p. 9; © Medford Historical Society Collection/CORBIS, p. 11; © Roger Viollet Collection/Getty Images, p. 12; © Hulton Archive/Getty Images, pp. 14, 100; Illustration from John Ransom's Andersonville diary, pp. 15, 177; Maine State Archives, p. 18 (#698A); National Archives, pp. 27 (top, 111-BA-1224), 28, 62 (165-A-446), 74 (165-A-445), 108 (111-B-3656), 111 (111-B-36), 131 (111-B-4146), 137 (111-B-1857), 173 (111-B-1857), 174 (bottom, 111-B-4146); Andersonville National Historic Site, National Park Service, pp. 29, 139; © Mary Evans/The Image Works, p. 34 (top); © Tria Giovan/CORBIS, p. 34 (bottom); Massachusetts Commandery Military Order of the Loyal Legion and the U.S. Army Military History Institute, p. 37; © Picture History, p. 41; © CORBIS, pp. 42–43, 49, 99, 118–119, 148; © North Wind Picture Archives, pp. 52, 81; From *Life and Death in Rebel Prisons* by Robert H. Kellogg, p. 70; United States Sanitary Commission records, Manuscripts and Archives Division, The New York Public Library, Astor, Lenox and Tilden Foundations, p. 79; © Kean Collection/Hulton Archive/Getty Images, p. 102; © MPI/Hulton Archive/Getty Images, p. 104; © akg-images/The Image Works, p. 122; © Stock Montage/Hulton Archive/Getty Images, p. 128; Picture Collection, The New York Public Library, Astor, Lenox and Tilden Foundations, p. 153; Mrs. John Henry Winder III, Winston-Salem, N.C., pp. 155, 179 (bottom); © JHP Travel/ Alamy, pp. 166, 171 (top); Courtesy of Georgia Archives, p. 169 (#sum-102); © Andre Jenny/Alamy, p. 171 (bottom left); © Jeff Greenberg/Lonely Planet Images/Getty Images, p. 171 (bottom right).

Front cover: © iStockphoto.com/Duncan Walker (top); © CORBIS (bottom).